AAT

Qualifications and Credit Framework (QCF)

AQ2013 (FA2015)
LEVEL 4 DIPLOMA IN ACCOUNTING

(QCF)
QUESTION BANK

Personal Tax

2015 Edition

For assessments from January 2016

Third edition August 2015
ISBN 9781 4727 2209 6

Previous edition August 2014
ISBN 9781 4727 09431

British Library Cataloguing-in-Publication Data
A catalogue record for this book is available from the British Library

Published by
BPP Learning Media Ltd
BPP House
Aldine Place
London W12 8AA

www.bpp.com/learningmedia

Printed in the United Kingdom by Martins of Berwick
Sea View Works
Spittal
Berwick-Upon-Tweed
TD15 1RS

CONTENTS

Introduction   v

Question and answer bank

Chapter tasks		Questions	Answers
1	The tax framework	3	69
2	Taxable income	7	73
3	Calculation of income tax	13	81
4	Employment income	19	89
5	Property income	33	103
6	Payment of tax and tax administration	41	109
7	Chargeable gains	51	115
8	Share disposals	61	125
9	Principal private residence	65	129
AAT AQ2013 Sample Assessment		133	147
BPP Practice Assessment 1		159	173
BPP Practice Assessment 2		185	201
BPP Practice Assessment 3		215	235
BPP Practice Assessment 4		249	267
BPP Practice Assessment 5		279	297

Taxation data	306

BPP note: Assessments under FA 2014 will cease to be available from 31 December 2015. Assessments under FA 2015 will be available from January 2016. This edition includes the provisions of FA 2015 and has been written specifically for students sitting AQ2013. Please ensure you check the date you intend to sit your assessment to ensure you are using the correct material.

A NOTE ABOUT COPYRIGHT

INTRODUCTION

This is BPP Learning Media's AAT Question Bank for Personal Tax. It is part of a suite of ground-breaking resources produced by BPP Learning Media for the AAT's assessments under the Qualification and Credit Framework.

The Personal Tax assessment will be **computer assessed**. As well as being available in the traditional paper format, this **Question Bank is available in an online environment** containing tasks similar to those you will encounter in the AAT's testing environment. BPP Learning Media believe that the best way to practise for an online assessment is in an online environment. However, if you are unable to practise in the online environment you will find that all tasks in the paper Question Bank have been written in a style that is as close as possible to the style that you will be presented with in your online assessment.

This Question Bank has been written in conjunction with the BPP Text, and has been carefully designed to enable learners to practise all of the learning outcomes and assessment criteria for the unit that makes up Personal Tax. It is fully up to date for Finance Act 2015 and reflects both the AAT's unit guide and the AAT sample assessments provided by the AAT.

This Question Bank contains these key features:

- Tasks corresponding to each chapter of the Text. Some tasks are designed for learning purposes, others are of assessment standard.

- The AAT's AQ2013 Sample Assessment and answers for Personal Tax and further BPP practice assessments.

The emphasis in all tasks and assessments is on the practical application of the skills acquired.

VAT

You may find tasks throughout this Question Bank that need you to calculate or be aware of a rate of VAT. This is stated at 20% in these examples and questions.

APPROACHING THE ASSESSMENT

When you sit the assessment it is very important that you follow the on screen instructions. This means you need to carefully read the instructions, both on the introduction screens and during specific tasks.

When you access the assessment you should be presented with an introductory screen with information similar to that shown below (taken from the introductory screen from the AAT's AQ2013 sample assessments for Personal Tax).

We have provided the following sample assessment to help you familiarise yourself with AAT's e-assessment environment. It is designed to demonstrate as many as possible of the question types you may find in a live assessment. It is not designed to be used on its own to determine whether you are ready for a live assessment.

You should attempt and aim to complete EVERY task.
Each task is independent. You will not need to refer to your answers to previous tasks.
Read every task carefully to make sure you understand what is required.

Please note that in this sample test only your responses to tasks 1, 2, 3, 4, 5, 9 and 11 are marked. Equivalents of tasks 6, 7, 8 and 10 will be human marked in the live assessment.

Where the date is relevant, it is given in the task data.
Both minus signs and brackets can be used to indicate negative numbers UNLESS task instructions say otherwise.
You must use a full stop to indicate a decimal point - for example, write 100.57 NOT 100,57 or 100 57

You may use a comma to indicate a number in the thousands, but you don't have to.
For example, 10000 and 10,000 are both OK.

Other indicators are not compatible with the computer-marked system.

Tax data is provided in this assessment. The data has been grouped into two parts to make it easier to display. You can access the data at any point by clicking on the buttons found in every task. The buttons will appear at the top of each task, and look like this:

When you click on a button, the table will appear in a pop-up window. You can then move or close the window. When you move on to a new task, you will have to re-open a window to see the data again.

The taxation data is also available below, in this introduction, and can be accessed at any time during the assessment by clicking on the introduction button on the bottom left of the assessment window.

The actual instructions will vary depending on the subject you are studying for. It is very important you read the instructions on the introductory screen and apply them in the assessment. You don't want to lose marks when you know the correct answer just because you have not entered it in the right format.

In general, the rules set out in the AAT sample assessments for the subject you are studying for will apply in the real assessment, but you should again read the information on this screen in the real assessment carefully just to make sure.

A full stop is needed to indicate a decimal point. We would recommend using minus signs to indicate negative numbers and leaving out the comma signs to indicate thousands, as this results in a lower number of key strokes and less margin for error when working under time pressure. Having said that, you can use whatever is easiest for you as long as you operate within the rules set out for your particular assessment.

You have to show competence in all sections of assessments and you should therefore complete all of the tasks. Don't leave questions unanswered.

In some assessments written or complex tasks may be human marked. In this case you are given a blank space or table to enter your answer into. You are told in the assessments which tasks these are.

If these involve calculations, it is a good idea to decide in advance how you are going to lay out your answers to such tasks by practising answering them on a word document, and certainly you should try all such tasks in this question bank and in the AAT's environment using the sample/practice assessments.

When asked to fill in tables, or gaps, never leave any blank even if you are unsure of the answer. Fill in your best estimate or enter a zero.

Note that for some assessments where there is a lot of scenario information or tables of data provided (eg tax tables), you may need to access these via 'pop-ups'. Instructions will be provided on how you can bring up the necessary data during the assessment.

Finally, take note of any task specific instructions once you are in the assessment. For example you may be asked to enter a date in a certain format or to enter a number to a certain number of decimal places.

Remember you can practise the BPP questions in this question bank in an online environment on our dedicated AAT Online page. On the same page is a link to the current AAT Sample Assessments as well.

If you have any comments about this book, please email nisarahmed@bpp.com or write to Nisar Ahmed, Head of Programme, BPP Learning Media Ltd, BPP House, Aldine Place, London W12 8AA.

SPECIFIC TOPIC LIST

The practice tasks are grouped according to the main topics assessed in Personal Tax. This table gives you a list of tasks dealing with specific topics to enable you to focus your task practice.

Topic	Practice tasks
Legislation and procedures	1.1, 1.2, 1.3
Duties and responsibilities of a tax practitioner	1.4, 1.5, 1.6, 1.7, 1.8
Types of income (non-savings, savings, dividend and exempt income)	2.1, 2.2, 2.4, 2.12, 2.13, 2.14
Calculation of taxable income	2.5, 2.6
Personal & age allowances	2.3, 2.7, 2.8, 2.9, 2.10, 2.11, 3.11
Income tax liability & payable	3.1, 3.2, 3.3, 3.4, 3.5, 3.6, 3.7, 3.8, 3.9, 3.10
Employed versus self-employed	4.1, 4.2
Car, fuel & van benefits	4.6, 4.7, 4.8, 4.9, 4.10, 4.26
Other employment benefits	4.11, 4.12, 4.13, 4.14, 4.15, 4.16, 4.17, 4.18, 4.19, 4.21
Allowable deductions from employment income	4.18, 4.22, 4.23, 4.24, 4.25
Calculation of employment income	4.3, 4.4, 4.5, 4.20
Employment tax return page	4.27
Calculation of property income	5.1, 5.2, 5.3, 5.4, 5.5, 5.6, 5.11, 5.13
Property income loss relief	5.7
Furnished holiday lets	5.8, 5.9, 5.10, 5.12, 5.14
Property income tax return pages	5.15
Filing date & payment of tax	6.1, 6.2, 6.9, 7.10
Record keeping	6.3
Penalties & interest	6.4, 6.5, 6.6, 6.7, 6.8
Chargeable disposals	7.1, 7.2, 7.3
Calculation of gains for individuals	7.4, 7.9, 7.12, 7.13
Capital losses	7.11, 7.14, 7.15
Capital gains tax payable	7.5, 7.6, 7.7, 7.8
Chattels	7.18, 7.19, 7.20, 7.21, 7.22
Connected persons	7.16, 7.17
Capital gains tax return pages	7.23
Share disposals	8.1, 8.2, 8.3, 8.4
Principal private residence relief	9.1, 9.2

Question bank

Chapter 1 – The tax framework

Task 1.1

The tax year 2015/16 runs from: (insert dates as xx/xx/xxxx)

06/04/2015

until

05/04/2016

···

Task 1.2

Tick to show whether the following statement is True or False.

Detailed regulations relating to tax law are contained in Statutory Instruments.

	✓
True	✓
False	

···

Task 1.3

Tick to show who the UK tax system is administered by.

	✓
Parliament	
Her Majesty's Revenue & Customs (HMRC)	✓
National Crime Agency (NCA)	
HM Customs & Excise	

···

Task 1.4

If you are employed by a firm of accountants, and suspect that one of your clients may be engaged in money laundering, whom should you inform about your suspicions?

	✓
HMRC	
Your firm's Money Laundering Reporting Officer	√
National Crime Agency	
Tax Tribunal	

Task 1.5

This style of task is human marked in the live assessment.

One of your clients has expressed concern that his personal tax information may be disclosed to members of his family, who are also clients of your firm. He feels that this would compromise his right to privacy in his personal affairs.

Write a note responding to this concern.

Task 1.6

Tick to show in which TWO of the following situations an accountant is able to disclose information about a client without their permission.

	✓
If the client is unwell and unable to respond to HMRC	
If money laundering is suspected	✓
Where it would be illegal not to disclose the information	✓
If the information is requested from a 'connected person'	

Task 1.7

The five fundamental principles on professional ethics for AAT members are:

Use the letters in the left column as a guide.

I	Integrity
O	Objectivity
Pc and dc	Professional competence & due care
C	Confidentiality
Pb	Professional behaviour

Task 1.8

Tick to show who you should inform about your suspicions if you are a sole practitioner, and suspect that one of your clients may be engaged in money laundering.

	✓
HMRC	
Another firm's Money Laundering Reporting Officer	
National Crime Agency	✓
Tax Tribunal	

Chapter 2 – Taxable income

Task 2.1

For each of the following sources of income, indicate whether it is non-savings income, savings income or dividend income by ticking the relevant box:

	Non-savings income	Savings income	Dividend income
Trading income	✓	☐	☐
Dividend received from a company	☐	☐	✓
Property income	✓	☐	☐
Building society interest	☐	✓	☐
Bank interest	☐	✓	☐
Pension income	✓	☐	☐
Employment income	✓	☐	☐
Interest from government stock ('gilts')	☐	✓	☐

Task 2.2

Olive received the following income in 2015/16.

Show the amount of income that she should enter on her tax return. If the income is exempt, enter 0.

(a) Bank account interest £160

£ _200_

(b) Premium bond prize £100

£ _0_

(c) Dividends received £540

£ _600_

Task 2.3

Bob was born in April 1934. His net income for 2015/16 is £28,500.

The age allowance Bob is entitled to for 2015/16 is:

£ | 10600

Task 2.4

For each of the following interest payments, indicate whether they are received gross, net of basic rate tax or are exempt from income tax by ticking the relevant box:

	Gross	Net	Exempt
Bank interest		✓	
Interest on an individual savings account (ISA)			✓
Building society interest		✓	
Interest from government stock ('gilts')	✓		

Task 2.5

You act for Jonty, who was born in July 1969. The following information is relevant for the year ended 5 April 2016:

(1) His salary was £38,730.

(2) His other income received was:

	£
Building society interest	80
Dividends	63

Jonty's taxable income for 2015/16 is:

£ | 18300

Task 2.6

Mr Betteredge has the following income for 2015/16:

	£
Salary for the year to 5 April 2016	15,665
Interest received (amount received shown):	
National Westminster Bank plc	457
ISA account	180
Nationwide Building Society account	400

Using the proforma layout provided, prepare a schedule of income for 2015/16, clearly showing the distinction between non-savings and savings income. If income is exempt, enter 0. Mr Betteredge's personal allowance should be deducted as appropriate. Fill in ALL the unshaded boxes, and add a 0 (zero) if necessary.

	Non-savings income £	Savings income £	Total £
Earnings	15665	0	
Bank deposit interest	0	500	
Building society interest	0	571,25	
ISA interest	0	0	
Net income	15665	1071,25	
Less personal allowance	10 600	1071,25	11 671,25
Taxable income	5065	1071,25	6136,25

Task 2.7

Hayley receives employment income of £95,000, bank interest of £1,600 and dividends of £4,500 in 2015/16.

(1) **Hayley's net income for 2015/16 is:**

£ | 102 000

(2) **The personal allowance that Hayley is entitled to for 2015/16 is:**

£ | 9600

Task 2.8

Max has net income of £115,000 for 2015/16. He made Gift Aid donations of £4,000 (gross) during the year.

Max's personal allowance for 2015/16 is:

£  5100

Task 2.9

Gavin was born in September 1932. In 2015/16, he receives pension income of £19,300, bank interest of £2,000 and dividends of £5,400.

(1) **Gavin's net income for 2015/16 is:**

£  28800

(2) **The age allowance that Gavin is entitled to for 2015/16 is:**

£  10610

Task 2.10

Sue was born in January 1938. In 2015/16, she receives pension income of £17,000, bank interest of £3,000 and dividends of £6,300.   3750   7000

(1) **Sue's net income for 2015/16 is:**

£ 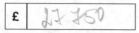 27 750

(2) **The age allowance that Sue is entitled to for 2015/16 is:**

£ 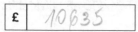 10635

Task 2.11

Ron was born in 1936. In 2015/16, he receives pension income of £33,000. He makes a Gift Aid donation of £1,500 (gross) in December 2015.

The age allowance that Ron is entitled to for 2015/16 is:

£ 10600

Task 2.12

From 6 April 2015 the maximum an individual can invest for the tax year in an ISA is:

£ 15240

....

Task 2.13

Tick to show whether the following statement is True or False.

Scholarships and educational grants are exempt as income of the student.

	✓
True	✓
False	

....

Task 2.14

Tick to show whether the following statement is True or False.

Damages received for an injury at work are only sometimes exempt from income tax, whereas damages paid on death are always exempt from income tax.

	✓
True	
False	✓

....

Chapter 3 – Calculation of income tax

Task 3.1

Guy receives bank interest of £7,500 in 2015/16. *9375*

Calculate the income tax liability on the bank interest ONLY assuming he has other non-savings income (net of personal allowance) of:

(1) **£1,000 (show whole pounds only)**

> £ |

(2) **£30,000 (show whole pounds only)**

> £ |

···

Task 3.2

6570

Holly is a higher rate taxpayer and receives a dividend of £5,913 in December 2015.

(1) **The tax credit attached to this dividend is:**

> £ | *657*

(2) **The rate of tax Holly will pay on this dividend (ignoring the effect of the tax credit) is:**

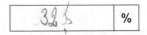

> *32.5* %

···

Task 3.3

You act for Deidre Watkins. Deidre was born in 1959 and has the following taxable income for 2015/16:

Non-savings income   £14,700
Savings income   £2,176
Dividend income   £1,766

Calculate Deidre's tax liability (show whole pounds only) on each source of income for 2015/16 as follows:

(1) **Non-savings income:**

£   2540

(2) **Savings income:**

£   135

(3) **Dividend income:**

£   177

Task 3.4

7800

Tony is a higher rate taxpayer and makes a Gift Aid donation of £6,000 in December 2015.

Tick to show the amount of Tony's basic rate band in 2015/16.

	✓
£37,785	
£31,785	
£39,285	✓
£36,585	

Task 3.5

Katy is an additional rate taxpayer and makes a Gift Aid donation of £4,000 in June 2015.

(1) **Katy's basic rate band for 2015/16 is:**

£   36 785

(2) **Katy's higher rate band for 2015/16 is:**

£   118 215

(3) **Katy's additional rate threshold for 2015/16 is:**

£   155 000

BPP
LEARNING MEDIA

Task 3.6

Rachel (born in 1966) received £13,000 bank interest in 2015/16. This is her only income.

Rachel's income tax liability for 2015/16 is:

£ _130_

....

Task 3.7

Richard has taxable non-savings income of £58,525 in 2015/16. He made pension contributions to his personal pension scheme of £10,800 during the year. Tax of £9,700 was deducted under the PAYE system.

Richard's income tax payable for 2015/16 is:

£ _4653_

....

Task 3.8

John Smith has the following income and outgoings for the tax year 2015/16:

	£
Salary (£8,500 tax deducted under PAYE)	50,000
Interest on a deposit account with the Scotia Bank	800 _1000_
Donation under the Gift Aid scheme made on 1 September 2015	2,400 _3000_
Dividends received on UK shares	900 _1000_

(1) **Using the proforma layout provided, prepare a schedule of income for 2015/16, clearly showing the distinction between non-savings, savings and dividend income. Fill in all the unshaded boxes. If an answer is zero input 0.**

	Non-savings income £	Savings income £	Dividend income £	Total £
Salary	50 000			
Dividend			1000	
Bank deposit interest		1000		
Net income	50000	1000	1000	52 000
Less personal allowance	(10600)			(10 600)
Taxable income	39 400	1000	1000	41 400

(2) **John's income tax liability for 2015/16 is:**

£ 9518

(3) **John's income tax payable for 2015/16 is:**

£ 718

Task 3.9

Jean Brown has the following income and outgoings for the tax year 2015/16:

	£
Salary (£48,500 tax deducted under PAYE)	155,000
Interest on a bank deposit account	2,400 3000
Personal pension contribution	8,000 10000
Dividends received on UK shares	4,500 5000

(1) **Using the proforma layout provided, prepare a schedule of income for 2015/16, clearly showing the distinction between non-savings, savings and dividend income. Fill in all the unshaded boxes. If an answer is zero input 0.**

	Non-savings income £	Savings income £	Dividend income £	Total £
Salary	155 000			
Dividend			5000	
Bank deposit interest		3000		
Net income	155 000	3 000	5 000	163 000
Less personal allowance	0	0	0	
Taxable income	155 000	3 000	5 000	163 000

(2) **Jean's income tax liability for 2015/16 is:**

£ 56 618

(3) **Jean's income tax payable for 2015/16 is:**

£ 7018

Task 3.10

This style of task is human marked in the live assessment.

During 2015/16 Joshua, who was born in 1934, has income as follows:

Pension income	£9,200
Bank interest received	£8,860 *11 075*
Dividends received	£9,000 *10 000*

Joshua made a Gift Aid donation of £1,500 in July 2015.

Calculate Joshua's total income tax (liability) for 2015/16, using the table given below. Show your answer in whole pounds.

	Total	NSI	SI	dividends
Pension	9200			
		9200		
Interest	11075	.	11075	
dividends	10000			10000
	30275	9200	11075	10000
PA	(10600)	(9200)	(1400)	
	19675	0	9675	10000
(9675 - 5000) x 20%	1935			
10000 x 10%	1000			
Tax liability.	1985			

....

Task 3.11

During 2015/16 Amanda, who was born in February1925, had pension income of £24,200. She also received dividends of £3,555. Amanda made a payment to charity under Gift Aid of £304 in December 2015.

What is Amanda's age allowance for 2015/16?

£	10 625

....

Chapter 4 – Employment income

Task 4.1

Show whether the following statement is True or False.

An employee has a contract for services.

	✓
True	
False	✓

....

Task 4.2

Peter undertakes some work for XYZ plc.

Tick which of the following factors would indicate that he either has a contract of service with XYZ plc or a contract for services.

Factor	Contract of service	Contract for services
Peter is entitled to paid holidays	✓	☐
Peter hires his own helpers	☐	✓
Peter takes substantial financial risks when undertaking work for XYZ plc	☐	✓
Peter does not have to rectify mistakes in his work at his own expense	✓	☐

....

Task 4.3

Emma is employed as a retail salesperson and provides you with the following information about what she has received from her employer:

(a) Monthly salary of £2,000 paid on the first of each month until September 2015, with a 2% increase starting from 1 October 2015

(b) Commission of £1,000 earned during a special sales event in March 2016, paid with the May 2016 salary

(c) Employer's contribution of 5% of salary on 31 March 2016 to company's occupational pension scheme

(d) Bonus of £1,200 received 30 April 2015, based on company's accounting profit for the year ended 31 March 2015

For each item, show the amount that will be taxable in 2015/16:

Use whole numbers, and if the answer is zero, write 0

Item	£
Salary	24480
Commission	0
Employer's pension contribution	0
Bonus	1200

Task 4.4

Show whether the following statement is True or False.

Tips received by a tour guide from customers are not earnings

	✓
True	
False	√

Task 4.5

A director of a company is entitled to a bonus for her employer's year ended 31 December 2015. The bonus is determined on 30 November 2015, credited to her director's account on 20 December 2015 and is actually paid to her on 6 January 2016.

The date of receipt of the bonus for employment income purposes is: (insert date as xx/xx/xxxx)

20/12/2015

Task 4.6

Mo was provided with a petrol engine car by her employer on 6 August 2015. The car cost the employer £13,500 and the list price of the car was £15,000. The car's CO_2 emissions were 188g/km.   32 %.

(1) **The cost of the car in the taxable benefit computation is:**

£ | 15000

(2) **The percentage used in the taxable benefit computation is:**

32 | %

(3) **The taxable benefit on the provision of the car is:**

£ | 3200

....

Task 4.7   10/12

Frank was provided with a new diesel engine car with a list price of £25,000 on 6 June 2015. The firm paid for all fuel (£2,300) without requiring any payment by Frank for fuel for private use. However, he was required to pay the firm £35 per month for the private use of the car itself. The car has CO_2 emissions of 163g/km.   30%.

(1) **The taxable benefit on the provision of the car is:**

£ | 5900

(2) **The taxable benefit on the provision of fuel is:**

£ | 5525

....

6250
(350)
5900

Task 4.8

Julian is provided with a company car for business and private use throughout 2015/16. The car had a list price of £11,500 when bought new in December 2014 although the company paid £10,000 for the car after a dealer discount. It has a diesel engine, with CO_2 emissions of 70g/km. The company pays for all running costs, including all fuel. Julian does not make any contribution for his private use of the car.

(1) The cost of the car in the taxable benefit computation is:

£ | 11 500

(2) The percentage used in the taxable benefit computation is:

12 | %

(3) The taxable benefit in respect of the provision of fuel for private use is:

£ | 2652

Task 4.9

Sarah works for XXM plc, and is provided with a company car for business and private use throughout 2015/16.

The car has a diesel engine with CO_2 emissions of 209g/km. It has a list price of £57,000. Sarah agreed to make a capital contribution of £6,000 towards the cost of the car. The company pays for all running costs, including all fuel. Sarah pays £50 a month towards the cost of private fuel – the actual cost of private fuel is about £90 a month.

(1) Tick to show which percentage is used in the taxable benefit computation.

	✓
27	
37	✓
39	
34	

(2) The taxable benefit in respect of the provision of the car is:

£ | 19 240

(3) The taxable benefit in respect of the provision of the fuel for private use is:

£ | 8477

Task 4.10

Francine is employed by Bale plc as a delivery driver and is supplied with a van, which she parks overnight at home. She uses the van to drive to the company's depot to pick up packages but otherwise is not allowed to use the van for her own private purposes. The company provides fuel for the van. The cost of fuel for driving the van from her home to the depot is £500 for 2015/16.

Tick to show the taxable benefit for Francine in respect of the van for 2015/16.

	✓
£3,150	
£3,744	
£3,650	
Nil	✓

Task 4.11

A camera costing £200 is bought by an employer for the private use by an employee on 6 April 2014. The camera is purchased by the employee for £50 on 6 April 2015, when its market value is £120.

The taxable benefit for 2015/16 is:

£	110

160
(50)
110.

Task 4.12

On 6 April 2015 an employer made a loan of £50,000 to an employee. The employee repaid £30,000 on 6 December 2015. The remaining £20,000 was outstanding at 5 April 2016. Interest paid during the year was £1,000. The official rate of interest was 3% throughout 2015/16.

(1) **Using the average method, the taxable benefit for 2015/16 is:**

1050
(1000)
50

£	50

(2) **Using the alternative method, the taxable benefit for 2015/16 is:**

£	200

50 000 x 8/12 x 3% = 1000
20000 x 4/12 v 3% = 200

1200 - 1000 = 200

Task 4.13

Tick to show whether the following statement is True or False.

If a loan of £7,000 to an employee is written-off and this is the only loan to the employee by the employer, there is no taxable benefit.

	✓
True	
False	✓

....

Task 4.14

(1) Vimal, who earns £30,000 a year, is given the use of a new television, costing £1,000, by his employer on 1 January 2014. Vimal subsequently buys the television from his employer for £100 on 1 January 2016 when it is worth £300.

The taxable benefit for 2015/16 is:

£ [ ]

(2) The television is used to keep Vimal entertained when living at 3 Sims Court, London EC1, a flat provided by his employer. The flat cost £120,000 five years ago when Vimal moved in, but due to a slump in property prices is now only worth £90,000. It has an annual value of £3,000. The official rate of interest is 3%.

The taxable benefit for 2015/16 is:

£ [ ]

....

Task 4.15

Giles receives a salary of £25,000 and has received the following benefits from his employer throughout 2015/16:

(1) Free medical insurance – the cost to the company is £385 per annum, although if Giles had taken this out privately he would have to pay £525.

(2) £55 per week of child care vouchers to be used towards the provision of crèche facilities for his child who attends a private nursery.

(3) A newspaper allowance of £20 per month.

Giles receives no income other than employment income.

The total taxable benefits for 2015/16 are:

£ 625

....

Task 4.16

Rita, a fashion designer for Daring Designs Ltd, was relocated from London to Manchester on 6 April 2015. Her annual salary is £48,000. She was reimbursed relevant relocation expenditure of £12,000. She was immediately provided with a house with an annual value of £4,000, for which her employer paid an annual rent of £3,500. Rita's employer provided ancillary services for the house in 2015/16 as follows:

	£
Electricity	700
Gas	1,200
Water	500
Council tax	1,300
Property repairs	3,500

The house had been furnished by Daring Designs Ltd immediately prior to Rita's occupation, at a cost of £30,000. On 6 October 2015 Rita bought all of the furniture from Daring Designs Ltd for £20,000 when its market value was £25,000.

Daring Designs Limited had made an interest free loan to Rita in 2014 of £10,000. No part of the loan has been repaid. Assume the official rate of interest is 3%.

(1) **The taxable benefit arising in respect of the accommodation provided for Rita in 2015/16 and purchase of the furniture is:**

£  21 200

(2) **The taxable benefit arising in respect of the relocation expenses is:**

£ 4000

(3) **The taxable benefit arising in respect of the interest free loan in 2015/16 is:**

£ 0

4000
700
1200
500
1300
3500

6/12 × 25000

Task 4.17

Jon's employer provided him with a flat throughout 2015/16. The employer had bought the flat for £97,000 on 1 April 2013. The annual value of the flat is £800. Jon pays £100 a month to his employer for the use of the flat.

Tick to show the total taxable accommodation benefit for 2015/16.

	✓
£800	
£1,460	
£260	√
£660	

Task 4.18

Petra uses her own car for business travel and her employer reimburses her 35p per mile. In 2015/16 Petra drove 13,000 business miles.

Tick to show what is Petra's taxable benefit or allowable expense in respect of the business mileage.

	✓
Taxable benefit of £700	
Allowable expense of £700	√
Allowable expense of £1,300	
Taxable benefit of £4,550	

Task 4.19

For an employee on an annual salary of £27,000, tick for each of the following benefits whether they would be taxable or exempt in 2015/16:

Item	Taxable	Exempt
Interest on loan of £2,000 (only loan provided)		✓
Removal costs of £6,000		✓
Use of pool car		✓
Reimbursement of business expenses under a dispensation		✓
One staff party costing £100 per head		✓
Accommodation provided to employee who is not required to live in it for the performance of employment	✓	
Provision of parking space at work		✓
Additional costs of home-working of £4 per week		✓
Long service award of £800 for 22 years service		✓
Accommodation provided to a caretaker for proper performance of his employment duties		✓
Work related training		✓
Provision of second mobile phone	✓	

Task 4.20

Selina is employed by JKL Ltd. She gives you with the following information about money she has received from her employer, and expenditure that she has incurred in relation to her employment in 2015/16:

(a) Annual salary £30,000

(b) Reimbursed business expenses of £600 – HMRC has agreed a dispensation

(c) Employee's contribution of 8% of salary to company's occupational pension scheme

(d) Membership of professional body of £150 paid by Selina

(e) Membership of fitness club of £300 paid by Selina – she often uses the club to meet new clients

(f) £50 donation to charity each month under the payroll deduction scheme

(g) £1,500 expenditure on smart clothes to wear to client meetings

Using the proforma layout provided, compute Selina's employment income for 2015/16. If an expense is not allowable enter 0. Both brackets and minus signs can be used to indicate negative numbers (the expenses). Fill in all of the unshaded boxes.

	£
Salary	30 000
Less allowable expenses:	
reimbursed expenses	(0)
pension contribution	(2400)
professional body membership	(150)
fitness club membership	—
charitable donation	(600)
clothing	—
Employment income 2015/16	26 850

Task 4.21

Lewis is required by his employer to move from Truro to Manchester.

The maximum amount of relocation expenses that his employer can pay without a taxable benefit arising is:

£ 8000

Task 4.22

In 2015/16 Dave earns £20,000 a year in his employment with BCD plc, and also receives dividend income of £6,300 from the company.

Tick to show the maximum pension contribution that Dave can make in 2015/16, on which he can obtain tax relief.

	✓
£3,600	
£20,000	✓
£26,300	
£27,000	

Task 4.23

Zara works for KJ Ltd. She incurs the following travelling expenses in 2015/16:

	£
Travel from her home in Preston to her workplace in Manchester	1,500
Travel to meet clients	300
Travel from her home in Preston to a temporary workplace in Birmingham (temporary period is 18 months)	1,800

Zara's qualifying travel expenses for 2015/16 are:

£ 2100

Task 4.24

Tick to show how the payroll deduction scheme works.

	✓
The employer deducts the contribution after calculating income tax under PAYE.	
The employer deducts basic rate tax from the contribution and the employee gets higher rate relief by extending the basic rate band in the tax computation.	
The employer deducts the contribution before calculating income tax under PAYE.	✓
The employer deducts basic rate tax from the contribution and there is no higher rate tax relief.	

Task 4.25

Tick to show how tax relief is given on an employee's contribution to an occupational pension scheme.

	✓
The pension contribution is paid net of basic rate tax, and higher rate tax relief is obtained by extending the basic rate band.	
The contribution is deducted from employment income as an allowable expense before tax is calculated under PAYE.	√

Task 4.26

This style of task is human marked in the live assessment.

You have received the following email from your client Martin Wilkes:

From:	MartinWilkes@boxmail.net
To:	AATStudent@boxmail.net
Sent:	12 March 2016 10:24
Subject:	Car

I have just received a promotion, and my employer is offering me a company car for business and personal use from 6 April 2016. My employer is getting a good deal on the car because I looked up the list price, which is £18,000, but they are only paying £14,000 after a discount from the dealer. I also noted that the car has CO_2 emissions of 173 g/km.

My employer will pay all the running costs of the car and will also provide all the fuel. I will pay £20 a month towards private fuel, but I think that my actual private fuel used would cost about £50.

Can you please explain all of the taxation aspects of the provision of this car as a taxable benefit? Is there any other information that you need to know?

Thanks,

Martin Wilkes

Reply to Martin's email, explaining to him the various taxation aspects that can apply to the provision of the car. Assume rates stay unchanged for future years.

From:	AATStudent@boxmail.net
To:	MartinWilkes@boxmail.net
Sent:	14 March 2016 12:29
Subject:	Car

Task 4.27

Your client, Jill Gilks, is employed by Beata plc. She has given you the following information about her employment:

Annual salary £60,000

Tax taken off pay £13,900

Company car – taxable benefit £5,200

Fuel benefit – taxable benefit £2,000

Expenses payments received £2,250 – this covers the exact amount spent by Jill on business travel. There is no dispensation agreed with HMRC

Professional subscription (paid by Jill) £225

Use this information to complete the Employment Page, which follows.

HM Revenue & Customs

Employment

Tax year 6 April 2015 to 5 April 2016

Your name	Your unique taxpayer reference (UTR)
Jill Giles	

Complete an *Employment* page for each employment or directorship

1 Pay from this employment - the total from your P45 or P60 - *before tax was taken off*

£ 60000 . 00

5 Your employer's name

Beata ore

2 UK tax taken off pay in box 1

£ – 13900 . 00

6 If you were a company director, put 'X' in the box

3 Tips and other payments not on your P60 - *read page EN 3 of the notes*

£ . 00

7 And, if the company was a close company, put 'X' in the box

4 PAYE tax reference of your employer (on your P45/P60)

/

8 If you are a part-time teacher in England or Wales and are on the Repayment of Teachers' Loans Scheme for this employment, put 'X' in the box

Benefits from your employment – use your form P11D (or equivalent information)

9 Company cars and vans - *the total 'cash equivalent' amount*

£ 5200 . 00

13 Goods and other assets provided by your employer - *the total value or amount*

£ . 00

10 Fuel for company cars and vans - *the total 'cash equivalent' amount*

£ 2000 . 00

14 Accommodation provided by your employer - *the total value or amount*

£ . 00

11 Private medical and dental insurance - *the total 'cash equivalent' amount*

£ . 00

15 Other benefits (including interest-free and low interest loans) - *the total 'cash equivalent' amount*

£ . 00

12 Vouchers, credit cards and excess mileage allowance

£ . 00

16 Expenses payments received and balancing charges

£ . 00

Employment expenses

17 Business travel and subsistence expenses

£ 2250 . 00

19 Professional fees and subscriptions

£ 225 . 00

18 Fixed deductions for expenses

£ . 00

20 Other expenses and capital allowances

£ . 00

ⓘ **Shares schemes, employment lump sums, compensation, deductions and Seafarers' Earnings Deduction** are on the *Additional information* pages enclosed in the tax return pack

SA102 2014   Tax return: Employment: Page E 1   HMRC 12/13

Chapter 5 – Property income

Task 5.1

9 months

Simran rents out a furnished house from 1 July 2015. The rent is £500 per month, payable on the first day of each month. She incurs the following costs relating to the rental:

	£
Electricity for 1 July 2015 to 31 March 2016	1,200
Water rates for 1 July 2015 to 31 March 2016	500
Insurance for 1 July 2015 to 30 June 2016	360 270

Simran claims the wear and tear allowance.

Tick to show what Simran's property income for 2015/16 is.

	✓
£2,080	
£1,990	
£2,040	
£2,130	✓

4500
(1 200)
(500)
400
(270)

··

Task 5.2

Julie received the following property income during 2015/16:   8 months

(1) Annual rental of £6,300 (payable in advance) from a furnished flat first let on 6 August 2015. Allowable expenses of £660 relate to the tax year. The tenant is responsible for paying water rates and council tax.

(2) £3,500 from letting a furnished room in her own home.

Julie claims the wear and tear allowance.

What amount of taxable property income does Julie have for 2015/16?

£   3120

··

4200
(660)
(420)

Task 5.3

Zelda lets out a house. Her accrued income and allowable expenses are as follows:

	Income £	Expenses £
2013/14	6,000	10,000
2014/15	8,000	5,500
2015/16	10,000	4,000

Zelda's property income for 2015/16 is:

£ _4500_

Task 5.4

On 1 October 2015 Nitin buys a badly dilapidated house for £350,000. During October 2015, he spends £40,000 on making the house habitable. He lets it furnished for £3,600 a month from 1 November 2015, but the tenant leaves on 31 January 2016. A new tenant moves in on 1 March 2016, paying £4,000 a month rent.

Water rates are £195 for the period 1 October 2015 to 31 March 2016, payable by Nitin. He also pays buildings insurance of £480 for the period from 1 October 2015 to 30 September 2016. He financed the purchase of £350,000 with a bank loan at 5% interest.

Nitin claims the wear and tear allowance. He spends £10,000 on furniture in October 2015.

Nitin's property income for 2015/16 is:

£

Task 5.5

Sinead starts to let out property on 1 July 2015.

(1) On 1 July 2015, she lets a house which she has owned for several years. The tenant is required to pay annual rent of £8,000, quarterly in advance. The house is let unfurnished. She incurs total allowable expenses of £1,200 in relation to this letting.

(2) On 1 December 2015, she lets out a house which she has bought. The tenant pays annual rent of £450 per month, payable on the first of each month. The house is let unfurnished. She incurs total allowable expenses of £2,000 in relation to this letting.

Sinead's property income for 2015/16 is:

£ _4155_

Task 5.6

Suzy let out a room in her house at a rent of £500 per month throughout 2015/16. Her allowable expenses for the year were £3,700.

Suzy's property income for 2015/16 is:

£ | *1750*

Task 5.7

In 2015/16, Sally makes a property income loss of £(5,000) on letting out Red Roofs, and property income profit of £3,000 on letting out Green Acres. Neither property is qualifying holiday accommodation. Sally also has employment income of £20,000 in 2015/16.

Sally can obtain loss relief by: Tick ONE box

	✓
Setting the loss of £(5,000) against her employment income in 2015/16	
Carrying forward the loss of £(5,000) against property income in 2016/17	
Setting the loss of £(5,000) first against the profit of £3,000 in 2015/16 and then carrying forward the balance of £(2,000) against property income in 2016/17	✓
Setting the loss of £(5,000) first against the profit of £3,000 in 2015/16 and then setting the balance of £(2,000) against employment income in 2015/16	

Task 5.8

A property can qualify as qualifying holiday accommodation if it is:

Available for letting to the public as holiday accommodation for at least | *250* | days in the tax year and actually let for at least | *105* | days during the same tax year and not normally occupied for periods of 'longer term occupation' (more than 31 consecutive days to the same person) for more than | *155* | days in a tax year.

Task 5.9

Tick to show whether the following statement is True or False.

Losses on qualifying holiday accommodation can be set against other income, not just property income.

	✓
True	
False	√

Task 5.10

Tick to show whether the following statement is True or False.

To be qualifying holiday accommodation, the property must be situated in the UK.

	✓
True	
False	√

Task 5.11

Olivia let out a room in her house at a rent of £40 per week throughout 2015/16. Her allowable expenses for the year were £2,500.

Olivia's property income loss for 2015/16 is (both brackets and minus signs can be used to indicate negative numbers):

£ (420)

Task 5.12

Tick to show which ONE of the following is not an advantage of property being qualifying holiday accommodation, as opposed to being taxed under the usual rules for letting furnished property.

	✓
The income qualifies as earnings for pension purposes	
The wear and tear allowance applies	√
Capital allowances are available on furniture	

Task 5.13

Len owns and lives in a house and he lets out a room to Kathy throughout 2015/16. Kathy pays Len £90 per week. Len estimates that the extra costs of renting the room to Kathy amount to £7 per week.

Tick to show the property income taxable on Len for 2015/16 assuming that he uses the rent a room scheme.

	✓
£90	
£430	√
£4,316	
£4,680	

Task 5.14

This style of task is human marked in the live assessment.

Your client Jessica wishes to invest some money which she inherited, by buying accommodation in a popular UK holiday resort. She believes there is a special treatment for income arising from letting out such a property.

Write brief notes explaining the conditions for the special treatment to apply, and the income tax advantages from this treatment.

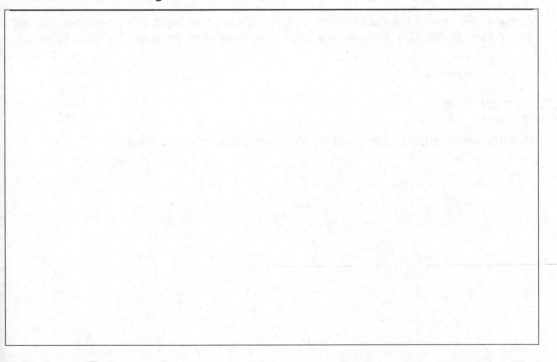

Task 5.15

Pierce Jones owns a flat that he rents out for £500 per calendar month, payable on the first day of each month. The property is let unfurnished. His other expenses for 2015/16 were:

	£
Electricity and gas	1,200
Water rates	400
Mortgage interest	3,200
Insurance	250

Use this information to complete the Property page, which follows.

UK property

Tax year 6 April 2015 to 5 April 2016

UK property details

Your name

PIERCE JONES

Your Unique Taxpayer Reference (UTR)

UK property details

1 Number of properties rented out

    1

2 If all property income ceased in 2015–16 and you do not expect to receive such income in 2016–17, put 'X' in the box and consider if you need to complete the *Capital gains summary* page

3 If you have any income from property let jointly, put 'X' in the box

4 If you are claiming Rent a Room relief and your rents are £4,250 or less nor £2,125 if let jointly), put 'X' in the box

Furnished holiday lettings (FHL) in the UK or European Economic Area (EEA)

Fill in one page for UK businesses and a separate page for EEA businesses. Please read the *UK property notes* before filling in boxes 5 to 19 if you have furnished holiday lettings

5 Income – *the amount of rent and any income for services provided to tenants*

    £ · 0 0

6 Rent paid, repairs, insurance and costs of services provided – *the total amount*

    £ · 0 0

7 Loan interest and other financial cost

    £ · 0 0

8 Legal, management and other professional fee

    £ · 0 0

9 Other allowable property expenses

    £ · 0 0

10 Private use adjustment – *if expenses include any amounts for non-business purposes*

    £ · 0 0

11 Balancing charges – *read the notes*

    £ · 0 0

12 Capital allowances – *read the notes*

    £ · 0 0

13 Adjusted profit for the year (if the amount in box 5 + box 10 + box 11 minus (boxes 6 to 9 + box 12) is positive)

    £ · 0 0

14 Loss brought forward used against this year's profit – *if you have a non-FHL property business loss read the notes on property losses*

    £ · 0 0

15 Taxable profit for the year (box 13 minus box 14)

    £ · 0 0

16 Loss for the year (if the amount in boxes 6 to 9 + box 12 minus (box 5 + box 10 + box 11) is positive)

    £ · 0 0

17 Total loss to carry forward

    £ · 0 0

18 If this business is in the EEA, put 'X' in the box – *read the notes*

19 If you want to make a period of grace election, put 'X' in the box

SA105 2014   Page UKP 1   HMRC 12/14
                                                              5013441 Z

39

Property income

Do not include furnished holiday lettings, Real Estate Investment Trust or Property Authorised Investment Funds dividends/distributions here.

20	Total rents and other income from property
	£ 6000 . 0 0

22	Premiums for the grant of a lease – from box E on the Working Sheet – *read the notes*
	£ . 0 0

21	Tax taken off any income in box 20
	£ . 0 0

23	Reverse premiums and inducements
	£ . 0 0

Property expenses

24	Rent, rates, insurance, ground rents etc
	£ 650 . 0 0

27	Legal, management and other professional fee
	£ . 0 0

25	Property repairs, maintenance and renewals
	£ . 0 0

28	Costs of services provided, including wages
	£ . 0 0

26	Loan interest and other financial cost
	£ 3200 . 0 0

29	Other allowable property expenses
	£ 1200 . 0 0

Calculating your taxable profit or loss

30	Private use adjustment – *read the notes*
	£ . 0 0

37	Rent a Room exempt amount
	£ . 0 0

31	Balancing charges – *read the notes*
	£ . 0 0

38	Adjusted profit for the year – from box O on the Working Sheet – *read the notes*
	£ 950 . 0 0

32	Annual Investment Allowance
	£ . 0 0

39	Loss brought forward used against this year's profit
	£ . 0 0

33	Business Premises Renovation Allowance (Assisted Areas only) – *read the notes*
	£ . 0 0

40	Taxable profit for the year (box 38 minus box 39
	£ 950 . 0 0

34	All other capital allowances
	£ . 0 0

41	Adjusted loss for the year – from box O on the Working Sheet – *read the notes*
	£ . 0 0

35	Landlord's Energy Saving Allowance
	£ . 0 0

42	Loss set off against 2015–16 total income – *this will be unusual – read the notes*
	£ . 0 0

36	10% wear and tear allowance – *for furnished residential accommodation only*
	£ . 0 0

43	Loss to carry forward to following year, including unused losses brought forward
	£ . 0 0

BPP
LEARNING MEDIA

Chapter 6 – Payment of tax and tax administration

Task 6.1

Tick to show the correct answer.

By which date should an individual normally submit his 2015/16 self assessment tax return if it is to be filed online?

	✔
31 January 2017	✔
5 April 2017	
31 October 2016	
31 December 2016	

Task 6.2

Gordon had income tax payable of £14,500 in 2014/15. His income tax payable for 2015/16 was £17,000.

How will Gordon settle his income tax payable for 2015/16?

	✔
The full amount of £17,000 will be paid on 31 January 2017	
Payments on account of £7,250 will be made on 31 January and 31 July 2016, with nothing due on 31 January 2017	
Payments on account of £8,500 will be made on 31 January and 31 July 2016 with nothing due on 31 January 2017	
Payments on account of £7,250 will be made on 31 January and 31 July 2016, with the balance of £2,500 being paid on 31 January 2017	✔

Task 6.3

Pat has property income and dividend income in 2015/16.

What is the latest date until which Pat must retain records of his income?

	✓
All records until 31 January 2018	
Property income until 31 January 2018, dividend income until 31 January 2022	
Property income until 31 January 2022, dividend income until 31 January 2018	
All records until 31 January 2022	✓

Task 6.4

Tick to show the correct answer.

The minimum penalty as a percentage of Potential Lost Revenue for a deliberate but not concealed error on a tax return, for which is there is an unprompted disclosure is:

	✓
0%	
20%	✓
30%	
35%	

Task 6.5

The maximum penalty per tax year for failing to keep records is:

£ 3000

Task 6.6

This style of task is human marked in the live assessment.

You have received the following letter from a client:

Dear Peter

Tax advice

I am employed as a general manager for Smith Brothers Ltd, based in Surrey. Up to now I have never had to complete a tax return, but recently I received a return from HMRC for the tax year to 5 April 2016, which I am not sure how to complete. I have arranged, with your secretary, to meet with you on Monday at 11.30 am.

I received and paid the following types of income and expenditure during the last tax year, but I am not sure what information or documents you might require to complete the return.

Income

Salary (£35,000 approximately)
Loan of a company car
Private medical insurance provided by the company
Bank interest
Building society interest

Interest from an Individual Savings Account

Payments

Contribution to a personal pension plan
Interest on a mortgage on my main residence
Subscription to the Institute of Personnel Managers

I would be grateful if you could inform me as to what I should bring with me to the meeting to help complete the tax return. Also could you answer the following questions?

(a)   When must the return be submitted to HMRC?
(b)   When will the tax be payable?
(c)   Are there any penalties if the deadlines in (a) and (b) are not met; if so what are they?
(d)   My wife earns £6,500 a year – does this need to be included on my return?

Yours sincerely

John Hunt

Reply to Mr Hunt's letter.

Question bank

44

Task 6.7

This style of task is human marked in the live assessment.

You have just submitted the tax return for 2015/16 for your client, Donald Icer, when you receive the following email from him:

From:	Dicer@hotnet.net
To:	AATStudent@boxmail.net
Sent:	30 November 2016
Subject:	Information

I know you have been working on my tax affairs, and I hope you haven't yet submitted the tax return, as I have just realised that there are some things that I haven't told you about.

During 2015/16, I received building society interest of £152 and interest from an ISA of £93. I also paid £100 to the National Trust, under Gift Aid.

I don't know if any of this is important, but I thought I should let you know anyway.

Thanks.

Donald

Reply to Donald's email informing him of:

(a) **The tax implications of each item**
(b) **The consequences of submitting an incorrect tax return**

You are not required to compute the income tax due as a result of these omissions. Donald does not pay income tax at the higher or additional rate.

From:	AATStudent@boxmail.net
To:	Dicer@hotnet.net
Sent:	1 December 2016
Subject:	Information

Task 6.8

This style of task is human marked in the live assessment.

You have just received the following email from your client, Clarissa, whom you have recently started to act for:

From:	clarissa@hotnet.net
To:	AATStudent@boxmail.net
Sent:	15 September 2016
Subject:	Worried

I am worried about my tax return for 2014/15 which I prepared myself. I have just realised that I didn't notify HMRC of interest of £420 on my government stocks for that year. I just forgot that I had the stock.

Can you please advise about what I should do and about any penalties or interest that I may incur? I was a basic rate taxpayer in 2014/15.

Thanks.

Clarissa

Reply to Clarissa's email.

From:	AATStudent@boxmail.net
To:	clarissa@hotnet.net
Sent:	17 September 2016
Subject:	Worried

Task 6.9

This style of task is human marked in the live assessment.

June has written to you with the following query:

'I have just had a tax bill from HMRC with the amount that I need to pay on 31 January 2017. You will remember that I started letting out some properties on 1 May 2015. The bill says that I need to pay £5,000 for 2015/16 which is the figure that you told me was my tax liability on my property income for that year. But it also says that I need to pay them £2,500 on 31 January 2017 as well. I don't understand this because my property income will probably be a lot less in 2016/17 than it was in 2015/16.

Please could you explain why I have to pay this extra amount and if there is anything I could do to reduce it?'

Make a list of the points you would make when responding to June's query.

Chapter 7 – Chargeable gains

Task 7.1

For the gain on the disposal of a capital asset to be a chargeable gain there must be a chargeable

> *disposal.*

of a chargeable

> *asset*

by a chargeable

> *person*

Task 7.2

Tick to show whether the following assets are chargeable assets or exempt assets for capital gains tax.

Item	Chargeable asset	Exempt asset
Car	☐	✓
A plot of land	✓	☐
Jewellery	✓	☐
Premium bonds	☐	✓
Government stock ('gilts')	☐	✓

Task 7.3

Tick to show which ONE of the following is not a chargeable disposal for capital gains purposes.

	✓
The gift of an asset	
The sale of part of an asset	
The transfer of an asset on death	✓
The sale of the whole of an asset	

Task 7.4

Kate purchased a freehold property for £40,000. Kate then spent £5,000 on a new roof for the property as the old roof was storm damaged prior to acquisition. She sold the property for £90,100 on 15 March 2016. Kate had not made any other disposals during 2015/16.

What is Kate's taxable gain for 2015/16?

	✓
£34,000	✓
£39,000	
£45,000	
£50,000	

Task 7.5

In November 2015, Lenny made chargeable gains of £20,100 and allowable losses of £3,560. He made no other disposals during 2015/16 and is a higher rate taxpayer.

(1) **Lenny's capital gains tax liability for 2015/16 is:**

£	1523

(2) **Lenny's capital gains tax liability is payable by: (insert date as xx/xx/xxxx)**

31/01/2017

Task 7.6

In November 2015, Larry made chargeable gains of £25,100 and allowable losses of £5,200. He made no other disposals during 2015/16. He has £4,000 of his basic rate tax band remaining.

Larry's capital gains tax liability for 2015/16 is:

£   2064

....

Task 7.7

Laura made chargeable gains of £5,100 in July 2015 and £17,500 in November 2015. In May 2015 she made allowable losses of £2,000. Laura has taxable income of £29,720 for 2015/16.

Laura's capital gains tax liability for 2015/16 is:

£   2454

....

Task 7.8

Lisa made chargeable gains of £27,100 in December 2015. She made no other disposals in the year. Her taxable income for 2015/16 was £25,820.

Lisa's capital gains tax liability for 2015/16 is:

£   3884

....

Task 7.9

Darren bought a 3 acre plot of land for £150,000. He sold two acres of the land at auction for £240,000. His disposal costs were £3,000. The market value of the one remaining acre at the date of sale was £60,000.

(1) **The cost of the land sold is:**

£   120 000

(2) **The chargeable gain on sale is:**

£   117 000

....

Task 7.10

Tick to show how a taxpayer will pay the capital gains tax due for 2015/16.

	✓
The full amount will be paid on 31 January 2017	✓
The full amount will be paid on 31 January 2016	
Payments on account will be made on 31 January and 31 July 2016, with the balance being paid on 31 January 2017	
Payments on account will be made on 31 January and 31 July 2015, with the balance being paid on 31 January 2016	

Task 7.11

Mattheus made gains of £18,200 and losses of £7,000 in 2015/16. He has losses brought forward of £5,000.

The losses to carry forward to 2016/17 are (do not use brackets or a minus sign):

£ 4900

Task 7.12

Mike inherited a valuable painting from a distant uncle in November 2007. The painting had cost his uncle £5,000 in January 2001 and was valued at £9,000 at the date of his death. Luckily for Mike, when he sold it in December 2015, the proceeds were £16,000.

Mike's chargeable gain on sale is:

£ 7000

Task 7.13

Luke sells one acre of land in August 2015 for £25,000. His disposal costs were £2,500. He had bought four acres of land for £15,000. The market value of the remaining land was £50,000 at the date of sale. The acquisition costs of the four acres of land were £1,500.

Luke's chargeable gain on sale is:

£ 17000

Task 7.14

Tick to show whether the following statement is True or False.

If an individual has allowable losses brought forward, these are only used to bring gains down to the annual exempt amount.

	✓
True	√
False	

....

Task 7.15

James has the following gains and losses arising from disposals of chargeable assets:

Tax year	2013/14	2014/15	2015/16
Gains	£2,000	£4,000	£13,400
Losses	£(14,000)	£(2,000)	£(2,000)

The maximum allowable loss carried forward to 2016/17 will be:

£   11 700

....

Task 7.16

Mary is married to Mike. Mike has a sister, Susan who is married to Simon. Susan and Simon have a daughter called Sarah.

Tick which ONE of the following is not a connected person in relation to Mary.

	✓
Mike	
Susan	
Simon	
Sarah	√

....

Task 7.17

Joanne gives an asset to her son in September 2015. There was an allowable loss on the disposal of £(3,000). Joanne also gave an asset to her daughter in October 2015. There was a chargeable gain of £5,000 on this disposal.

Tick to show whether the following statement is True or False.

The loss of £(3,000) can be set against the gain of £5,000.

	✓
True	
False	✓

Task 7.18

Xena bought a vase for £1,500 and sold it in October 2015 for £6,500, incurring expenses of sale of £130.

Her chargeable gain on sale is:

£ 833

Task 7.19

Jolyon purchased a gold ring for £7,000. He sold it in January 2016 for £3,000. The expenses of sale were £125.

Jolyon's allowable loss is (do not use brackets or a minus sign):

£ 1125

Task 7.20

Rowenna bought a necklace for £4,000. She sold it in September 2015 for £5,500.

Tick to show whether the following statement is True or False.

Rowenna has a chargeable gain on sale of £1,500.

	✓
True	
False	✓

Task 7.21

Gilda purchased a picture for £3,500 and sold it in September 2015 for £7,500, incurring £300 expenses of sale.

Tick to show the chargeable gain on sale of the picture.

	✓
£1,200	
£2,000	
£2,500	✓
£3,700	

....

Task 7.22

Mark purchased an antique vase for £9,000. He sold the vase in August 2015 at auction for £4,500 net of auctioneer's fees of £500.

Mark's allowable loss is (both minus signs and brackets can be used to indicate negative numbers):

£  3500

....

Task 7.23

Your client, Isabel Redding, has given you the following information about her capital gains position for 2015/16:

Asset sold	Proceeds	Cost
Listed shares in Vodafone plc	£7,000	£9,500
Unlisted shares in Willard Ltd	£5,000	£2,800
Plot of land	£30,000	£13,100

She also has losses of £(1,750) brought forward from 2014/15.

Using this information, complete the capital gains tax summary on the next two pages.

 **HM Revenue & Customs**

Capital gains summary
Tax year 6 April 2015 to 5 April 2016

1	Your name	2	Your Unique Taxpayer Reference (UTR)
	ISABEL REDDING		

Summary of your enclosed computations

Please read the *Capital gains summary notes* before filling in this section. **You must enclose your computations,** including details of each gain or loss, as well as filling in the boxes.

ⓘ To get notes and helpsheets that will help you fill in this form, go to hmrc.gov.uk/selfassessmentforms

3 Total gains *(Boxes 21 + 27 + 33 + 34)*
£ 19100 00

4 Gains qualifying for Entrepreneurs' Relief (but excluding gains deferred from before 23 June 2010) – *read the notes*
£ • 0 0

5 Gains invested under Seed Enterprise Investment Scheme and qualifying for exemption – *read the notes*
£ • 0 0

6 Total losses of the year – *enter '0' if there are none*
£ 2500 00

7 Losses brought forward and used in the year
£ 1750 • 00

8 Adjustment to Capital Gains Tax – *read the notes*
£ • 0 0

9 Additional liability for non-resident or dual resident trusts
£ • 0 0

10 Losses available to be carried forward to later years
£ • 0 0

11 Losses used against an earlier year's gain (special circumstances apply – *read the notes*)
£ • 0 0

12 Losses used against income – amount claimed against 2015-16 income – *read the notes*
£ • 0 0

13 Amount in box 12 relating to shares to which Enterprise Investment Scheme/Seed Enterprise Investment Scheme relief is attributable
£ • 0 0

14 Losses used against income – amount claimed against 2014-15 income – *read the notes*
£ • 0 0

15 Amount in box 14 relating to shares to which Enterprise Investment Scheme/Seed Enterprise Investment Scheme relief is attributable
£ • 0 0

16 Income losses of 2015-16 set against gains
£ • 0 0

17 Deferred gains from before 23 June 2010 qualifying for Entrepreneurs' Relief
£ • 0 0

 BPP LEARNING MEDIA

Listed shares and securities

18 Number of disposals - *read the notes*

`1`

19 Disposal proceeds

£ `7000` · `0 0`

20 Allowable costs (including purchase price)

£ `9500` · `0 0`

21 Gains in the year, before losses

£ `0` · `0 0`

22 If you are making any claim or election, put 'X' in the box

23 If your computations include any estimates or valuations, put 'X' in the box

Unlisted shares and securities

24 Number of disposals - *read the notes*

`1`

25 Disposal proceeds

£ `5000` · `0 0`

26 Allowable costs (including purchase price)

£ `2800` · `0 0`

27 Gains in the year, before losses

£ `2200` · `0 0`

28 If you are making any claim or election, put 'X' in the box

29 If your computations include any estimates or valuations, put 'X' in the box

Property and other assets and gains

30 Number of disposals

`1`

31 Disposal proceeds

£ `30000` · `0 0`

32 Allowable costs (including purchase price)

£ `13100` · `0 0`

33 Gains in the year, before losses

£ `16900` · `0 0`

34 Attributed gains where personal losses cannot be set off

£ · `0 0`

35 If you are making any claim or election, put 'X' in the box

36 If your computations include any estimates or valuations, put 'X' in the box

Any other information

37 Please give any other information in this space

Chapter 8 – Share disposals

Task 8.1

On 17 January 2016 Lionel sold 10,000 ordinary shares in Old plc. He had originally purchased 12,000 shares in Old plc on 10 May 2008, and purchased another 8,000 shares on 24 January 2016.

Tick to show how Lionel's disposal of 10,000 shares in Old plc will be matched with his acquisitions.

	✓
Against 10,000 of the shares purchased on 10 May 2008	
Against 5,000 of the shares purchased on 24 January 2016 and then against 5,000 of the shares purchased on 10 May 2008	
Against 10,000 of the total shareholding of 20,000 shares	
Against the 8,000 shares purchased on 24 January 2016 and then against 2,000 of the shares purchased on 10 May 2008	√

Task 8.2

Mr Stevens sold 5,000 ordinary shares in JKL plc for £20,000 on 10 August 2015. He bought 6,000 shares in JKL plc for £9,000 on 15 July 2014 and another 1,000 shares for £4,200 on 16 August 2015.

His net chargeable gain on sale is:

£ 9,800

Task 8.3

This style of task is human marked in the live assessment.

Eloise's dealings in Moo plc were as follows:

	No. of shares	Cost/proceeds
		£
10 February 2001	12,000	18,000
20 September 2008	Bonus issue of 1 for 4	Nil
15 March 2016	(2,000)	8,000

Using the proforma layout provided, calculate Eloise's gain on sale. Fill in all the unshaded boxes and if the answer is zero insert '0'. Both minus signs and brackets can be used to indicate negative numbers.

Share pool

	No. of shares	Cost £
10 February 2001	12 000	18 000
20 September 2008 Bonus 1:4	3 000	0
	15 000	18 000
15 March 2016 Disposal	(2000)	(2400)
	13 000	15 600

Gain on sale

	£
Proceeds	8000
Less cost	(2400)
Gain	5600

Task 8.4

This style of task is human marked in the live assessment.

Mark sold 10,000 of his shares in AC plc on 4 November 2015 for £60,000. The shares had been acquired as follows:

	No. of shares	Cost £
9 December 2001	12,000	4,400
12 October 2005 (Rights issue 1:3 at £5)		
10 November 2015 ✓	2,000	11,500

Calculate Mark's total chargeable gain on sale. All workings must be shown. If the answer is zero insert '0'. Both minus signs and brackets can be used to indicate negative numbers.

	Shares	Cost
	12,000	4400
	4000	20000
	2000	11 500
Total	18 000	35 900
4/11/15 disposal	(10 000)	(23 700)
2000	8000	12 200
Proceeds	60000	
Less cost	(13 700)	
Gain	36 300	
Proceeds 2000/10000 × 60000= 12000		
8000/10000 × 60000 = 48000		
Cost 8000/16000 × 24400 12200		

Chapter 9 – Principal private residence

Task 9.1

Nicole is selling her main residence, which she has owned for 25 years. She lived in the house for the first 8 years of ownership, let the property for the next 5 years whilst she was posted abroad by her employer, returned to live in the house for the next 2 years, and then moved out for the remainder of her period of ownership.

Tick to show what fraction of her gain will be exempt under the private residence exemption.

$8 + 5 + 2 + 1.5$

	✓
16.5/25	✓
8.5/25	
15.5/25	
11.5/25	

$10/18$

Task 9.2

$34. + 54 + 0,54 + 1,5$

Mr Fox bought a house on 1 August 1997 for £50,000. He lived in the house until 31 July 2000. He then went abroad to work as a self-employed engineer until 31 July 2005. He lived in the house again until 31 January 2006, when he moved out.

Mr Fox sold the house on 31 July 2015 for £180,000.

Using the proforma layout provided, calculate the chargeable gain on sale.

	£
Proceeds	180 000
Less cost	(50 000)
Gain before PPR exemption	130 000
Less PPR exemption	72 222
Chargeable gain	57 778

Answer bank

Answer bank

Chapter 1

Task 1.1

The tax year 2015/16 runs from:

06/04/2015

until

05/04/2016

···

Task 1.2

Detailed regulations relating to tax law are contained in Statutory Instruments.

	✓
True	✓
False	

···

Task 1.3

The UK tax system is administered by:

	✓
Parliament	
Her Majesty's Revenue & Customs (HMRC)	✓
National Crime Agency (NCA)	
HM Customs & Excise	

···

Task 1.4

If you are employed by a firm of accountants, and suspect that one of your clients may be engaged in money laundering, whom should you inform about your suspicions?

	✓
HMRC	
Your firm's Money Laundering Reporting Officer	✓
National Crime Agency	
Tax Tribunal	

Task 1.5

Please be assured that an ethical guideline of confidentiality applies in your dealings with our firm.

This guideline means that your personal information will remain confidential, unless you give us authority to disclose information to third parties such as members of your family.

Task 1.6

An accountant is able to disclose information about a client without their permission in TWO of the following situations.

	✓
If the client is unwell and unable to respond to HMRC	
If money laundering is suspected	✓
Where it would be illegal not to disclose the information	✓
If the information is requested from a 'connected person'	

Task 1.7

The five fundamental principles on professional ethics for AAT members are:

I	Integrity
O	Objectivity
Pc and dc	Professional competence and due care
C	Confidentiality
Pb	Professional behaviour

Task 1.8

If you are a sole practitioner, and suspect that one of your clients may be engaged in money laundering, whom should you inform about your suspicions?

	✓
HMRC	
Another firm's Money Laundering Reporting Officer	
National Crime Agency	✓
Tax Tribunal	

Answer bank

Chapter 2

Task 2.1

	Non-savings income	Savings income	Dividend income
Trading income	✓		
Dividend received from a company			✓
Property income	✓		
Building society interest		✓	
Bank interest		✓	
Pension income	✓		
Employment income	✓		
Interest from government stock ('gilts')		✓	

Task 2.2

(a) Bank account interest £160

£	200

£160 × 100/80

(b) Premium bond prize £100

£	0

Premium bond prizes are exempt income

(c) Dividends received £540

£	600

£540 × 100/90

Task 2.3

The age allowance Bob is entitled to for 2015/16 is:

£	10,600

	£
Age allowance (born before 6/4/1938)	10,660
Less ½ × £(28,500 – 27,700)	(400)
Age allowance	10,260
Minimum allowance	10,600

Task 2.4

	Gross	Net	Exempt
Bank interest		✓	
Interest on an individual savings account (ISA)			✓
Building society interest		✓	
Interest from government stock ('gilts')	✓		

Task 2.5

Jonty's taxable income for 2015/16 is:

£	28,300

	Non-savings income £	Savings income £	Dividend income £	Total £
Earnings	38,730			
Building society interest (£80 × 100/80)		100		
Dividends (£63 × 100/90)			70	
Net income	38,730	100	70	38,900
Less personal allowance	(10,600)			(10,600)
Taxable income	28,130	100	70	28,300

Task 2.6

	Non-savings income £	Savings income £	Total £
Earnings	15,665	0	
Bank deposit interest (£457 × 100/80)	0	571	
Building society interest (£400 × 100/80)	0	500	
ISA interest: exempt	0	0	
Net income	15,665	1,071	16,736
Less personal allowance	(10,600)	0	(10,600)
Taxable income	5,065	1,071	6,136

Task 2.7

(1) Hayley's net income for 2015/16 is:

£	102,000

	Non-savings income £	Savings income £	Dividend income £	Total £
Employment income	95,000			
Bank interest (£1,600 × 100/80)		2,000		
Dividends (£4,500 × 100/90)			5,000	
Net income	95,000	2,000	5,000	102,000

(2) The personal allowance that Hayley is entitled to for 2015/16 is:

£	9,600

	£
Net income	102,000
Less income limit	(100,000)
Excess	2,000
Personal allowance	10,600
Less half excess	(1,000)
	9,600

Task 2.8

Max's personal allowance for 2015/16 is:

£	5,100

	£
Net income	115,000
Less gift Aid donations (gross)	(4,000)
Adjusted net income	111,000
Less income limit	(100,000)
Excess	11,000
Personal allowance	10,600
Less half excess	(5,500)
	5,100

··

Task 2.9

(1) Gavin's net income for 2015/16 is:

£	27,800

	Non-savings income £	Savings income £	Dividend income £	Total £
Pension income	19,300			
Bank interest (£2,000 × 100/80)		2,500		
Dividends (£5,400 × 100/90)			6,000	
Net income	19,300	2,500	6,000	27,800

(2) The age allowance that Gavin is entitled to for 2015/16 is:

£	10,610

	£
Net income	27,800
Less income limit	(27,700)
Excess	100
Age allowance (born before 6/4/1938)	10,660
Less half excess	(50)
	10,610

Task 2.10

(1) Sue's net income for 2015/16 is:

£	27,750

	Non-savings income £	Savings income £	Dividend income £	Total £
Pension income	17,000			
Bank interest (£3,000 × 100/80)		3,750		
Dividends (£6,300 × 100/90)			7,000	
Net income	17,000	3,750	7,000	27,750

(2) The age allowance that Sue is entitled to for 2015/16 is:

£	10,635

	£
Net income	27,750
Less income limit	(27,700)
Excess	50
Age allowance (born before 6/4/1938)	10,660
Less half excess	(25)
	10,635

Task 2.11

The age allowance that Ron is entitled to for 2015/16 is:

£	10,600

	£
Net income	33,000
Less Gift Aid donation (gross)	(1,500)
Adjusted net income	31,500
Less income limit	(27,700)
Excess	3,800
Age allowance	10,660
Less half excess	(1,900)
	8,760
Minimum allowance	10,600

Task 2.12

From 6 April 2015 the maximum an individual can invest for the tax year in an ISA is:

£	15,240

Task 2.13

Scholarships and educational grants are exempt as income of the student.

	✓
True	✓
False	

Task 2.14

The statement is false. Damages received for both injury and death are always exempt from income tax.

	✓
True	
False	✓

Chapter 3

Task 3.1

(1) Guy's income tax liability on the bank interest is:

£	1,075

	Non-savings income £	Savings income £	Total £
Bank interest (£7,500 × 100/80)		9,375	
Taxable income (net of PA)	1,000	9,375	10,375

Tax on bank interest only:

£5,000 – £1,000 = £4,000 × 0%	0
£9,375 – £4,000 = £5,375 × 20%	1,075
Income tax liability on the bank interest	1,075

(2) Guy's income tax liability on the bank interest is:

£	3,393

	Non-savings income £	Savings income £	Total £
Bank interest (£7,500 × 100/80)		9,375	
Taxable income (net of PA)	30,000	9,375	39,375

Tax on bank interest only:

£31,785 – £30,000 = £1,785 × 20%	357
£9,375 – £1,785 = £7,590 × 40%	3,036
Income tax liability on the bank interest	3,393

Task 3.2

(1) The tax credit attached to this dividend is:

£	657

£5,913 net dividend × 100/90 = £6,570 gross dividend

Tax credit is £6,570 × 10% = £657

Alternatively a quicker way to calculate the tax credit is to multiply the net dividend received by 10/90 which gives £5,913 × 10/90 = £657

(2) The rate of tax Holly will pay on this dividend (ignoring the effect of the tax credit) is:

32.5	%

Task 3.3

(1) Non-savings income:

£	2,940

(2) Savings income:

£	435

(3) Dividend income:

£	177

	Non-savings income £	Savings income £	Dividend income £	Total £
Taxable income	14,700	2,176	1,766	18,64
Tax on non-savings income:	£14,700 × 20%		2,940	
Tax on savings income:	£2,176 × 20%		435	
Tax on dividend income:	£1,766 × 10%		177	
Income tax liability			3,552	

Task 3.4

	✓
£37,785	
£31,785	
£39,285	✓
£36,585	

Basic rate band extended by the gross Gift Aid donation, ie £(6,000 × 100/80) = £7,500

£31,785 + £7,500 = £39,285

Task 3.5

(1) Katy's basic rate band for 2015/16 is:

£ | 36,785

Basic rate band extended by the gross Gift Aid donation, ie £(4,000 × 100/80) = £5,000

£31,785 + £5,000

(2) Katy's higher rate band for 2015/16 is:

£ | 118,215

(3) Katy's additional rate threshold for 2015/16 is:

£ | 155,000

Additional rate threshold = £36,785 + £118,215 (or £150,000 + £5,000)

Task 3.6

Rachel's income tax liability for 2015/16 is:

£	130

	£
Net income £13,000 × 100/80	16,250
Less personal allowance	(10,600)
Taxable income	5,650

	£
£5,000 × 0%	0
£5,650 − 5,000 = £650 × 20%	130
Income tax liability	130

Task 3.7

Richard's income tax payable for 2015/16 is:

£	4,653

	Non-savings income
	£
Taxable income	58,525

	£
Tax £31,785 × 20%	6,357
£13,500 (extended by £10,800 x 100/80) × 20%	2,700
£45,285	
£13,240 × 40%	5,296
£58,525	
Income tax liability	14,353
Less tax suffered at source (PAYE)	(9,700)
Income tax payable	4,653

Task 3.8

(1)

	Non-savings income £	Savings income £	Dividend income £	Total £
Salary	50,000	0	0	
Dividend £900 × 100/90	0	0	1,000	
Bank deposit interest £800 × 100/80	0	1,000	0	
Net income	50,000	1,000	1,000	52,000
Less personal allowance	(10,600)	0	0	(10,600)
Taxable income	39,400	1,000	1,000	41,400

(2) John's income tax liability for 2015/16 is:

£	9,529

(3) John's income tax payable for 2015/16 is:

£	729

	£
Tax on non-savings income	
£31,785 × 20%	6,357
£3,000 (extended band: Gift Aid £2,400 × 100/80) × 20%	600
£4,615 (£39,400 − 31,785 − 3,000) × 40%	1,846
Tax on savings income	
£1,000 × 40%	400
Tax on dividend income	
£1,000 × 32.5%	326
Income tax liability	9,529
Less tax credit on dividend income (£1,000 × 10%)	(100)
Less tax suffered on bank interest (£1,000 × 20%)	(200)
Less PAYE (given)	(8,500)
Income tax payable	729

Task 3.9

(1)

	Non-savings income £	Savings income £	Dividend income £	Total £
Salary	155,000	0	0	
Dividend £4,500 × 100/90	0	0	5,000	
Bank deposit interest £2,400 × 100/80	0	3,000	0	
Net income	155,000	3,000	5,000	163,000
Less personal allowance	0	0	0	0
Taxable income	155,000	3,000	5,000	163,000

The net income is in excess of £121,200 so the personal allowance is reduced to nil.

(2) Jean's income tax liability for 2015/16 is:

£	56,618

(3) Jean's income tax payable for 2015/16 is:

£	7,018

	£
Tax on non-savings income	
£31,785 × 20%	6,357
£10,000 (extended band: pension) £8,000 × 100/80 × 20%	2,000
£113,215 × 40%	45,286
Tax on savings income	
£3,000 × 40%	1,200
Tax on dividend income	
£2,000 × 32.5%	650
£3,000 × 37.5%	1,125
Income tax liability	56,618

	£
Income tax liability b/fwd	56,618
Less tax deducted at source	
Tax credit on dividend income (£5,000 × 10%)	(500)
Tax suffered on bank interest (£3,000 × 20%)	(600)
PAYE (given)	(48,500)
Income tax payable	7,018

Note. Additional rate threshold is increased by £10,000 to £160,000. Therefore only £3,000 of the dividend income is taxed at the additional rate.

Task 3.10

	Non-savings income £	Savings income £	Dividend income £	Total £
Pension income	9,200			
Bank interest £8,860 × 100/80		11,075		
Dividends £9,000 × 100/90			10,000	
Net income	9,200	11,075	10,000	30,275
Personal allowance (W)	(9,200)	(1,400)		(10,600)
Taxable income	Nil	9,675	10,000	19,675
Tax on savings income:				
£5,000 × 0%		0		
£4,675 (£9,675 – £5,000) × 20%		935		
Tax on dividend income:				
£10,000 × 10%		1,000		
Income tax liability		1,935		

Working

	£
Net income	30,275
Less Gift Aid donation (£1,500 × 100/80)	(1,875)
Adjusted net income	28,400
Less income limit	(27,700)
Excess	700
Age allowance	10,660
Less half excess	(350)
Adjusted age allowance	10,310
Minimum allowance	10,600

Task 3.11

Amanda's age allowance for 2015/16 is:

£	10,625

	Non-savings income	Dividend income	Total
	£	£	£
Pension income	24,200		
Dividend income (£3,555 × 100/90)		3,950	
Net income	24,200	3,950	28,150

	£
Net income	28,150
Less Gift Aid donation (£304 × 100/80)	(380)
Adjusted net income	27,770
Less income limit	(27,700)
Excess	70

	£
Age allowance	10,660
Less half excess	(35)
Adjusted age allowance	10,625

BPP
LEARNING MEDIA

Chapter 4

Task 4.1

	✓
True	
False	✓

An employee has a contract of service.

Task 4.2

Factor	Contract of service	Contract for services
Peter is entitled to paid holidays	✓	
Peter hires his own helpers		✓
Peter takes substantial financial risks when undertaking work for XYZ plc		✓
Peter does not have to rectify mistakes in his work at his own expense	✓	

Task 4.3

Item	£
Salary	24,280
Commission	0
Employer's pension contribution	0
Bonus	1,200

Salary paid on the first of each month, therefore received in 2015/16 as follows:

1 May 2015 to 1 September 2015 = 5 × £2,000 = £10,000

1 October 2015 to 1 April 2016 = 7 × £2,000 × 102% = £14,280

Salary = £10,000 + £14,280 = £24,280

Task 4.4

	✓
True	
False	✓

Tips received by a tour guide from customers are earnings. Note that earnings can include money received other than from the employer.

Task 4.5

The date of receipt of the bonus for employment income purposes is:

20/12/2015

Task 4.6

(1) The cost of the car in the taxable benefit computation is:

£	15,000

(2) The percentage used in the taxable benefit computation is:

32	%

The CO_2 emissions of the car are 185g/km (rounded down to the nearest five).

Amount over baseline figure: 185 – 95 = 90 g/km

Divide 90 by 5 = 18

The taxable percentage is 14% + 18% = 32%

(3) The taxable benefit on the provision of the car is:

£	3,200

32% × £15,000 × 8/12 (6 August 2015 to 5 April 2016)

Task 4.7

(1) The taxable benefit on the provision of the car is:

£ | 5,900

Round down CO_2 emissions to 160 g/km

Amount above baseline: 160 – 95 = 65 g/km

Divide 65 by 5 = 13

Taxable % = 14% + 13% + 3% (diesel) = 30%

	£
£25,000 × 30% × 10/12	6,250
Less employee contribution (10 × £35)	(350)
Taxable benefit of car	5,900

(2) The taxable benefit on the provision of fuel is:

£ | 5,525

£22,100 × 30% × 10/12 = £5,525

Task 4.8

(1) The cost of the car in the taxable benefit computation is:

£ | 11,500

(2) The percentage used in the taxable benefit computation is:

12 | %

As CO_2 emissions are from 51g to 75g/km = 9% + 3% (diesel)

(3) The taxable benefit in respect of the provision of fuel for private use is:

£ | 2,652

£22,100 × 12%

Task 4.9

(1) The percentage used in the taxable benefit computation is:

	✓
27	
37	✓
39	
34	

Round down CO_2 emissions to 205 g/km

Amount above baseline: 205 – 95 = 110 g/km

Divide 110 by 5 = 22

Taxable % = 14% + 22% + 3% (diesel) = 39%, max 37%

(2) The taxable benefit in respect of the provision of the car is:

£	19,240

	£
List price	57,000
Less capital contribution paid by employee (max)	(5,000)
Cost of car	52,000
Car benefit £52,000 × 37%	19,240

(3) The taxable benefit in respect of the provision of fuel for private use is:

£	8,177

£22,100 × 37% = £8,177 There is no reduction for part reimbursement of private fuel.

Task 4.10

£3,150	
£3,744	
£3,650	
Nil	✓

There is no taxable benefit because there is no private use of the van – travel from home to work is not private use for vans.

....

Task 4.11

The taxable benefit for 2015/16 is:

£	110

The benefit taxable in 2014/15 was 20% × £200 = £40

The benefit taxable in 2015/16 will be the greater of:

		£	£
(a)	Market value at acquisition by employee	120	
(b)	Original market value	200	
	Less benefit for use in 2014/15	(40)	
		160	
	ie		160
	Less price paid by employee		(50)
	Taxable benefit 2015/16		110

....

Task 4.12

(1)   Using the average method, the taxable benefit for 2015/16 is:

£ | 50

	£
3% × (50,000 + 20,000)/2	1,050
Less interest paid	(1,000)
Taxable benefit	50

(2)   Using the alternative method, the taxable benefit for 2015/16 is:

£ | 200

	£
£50,000 × 8/12 × 3%	1,000
(6 April 2015 to 5 December 2015)	
£20,000 × 4/12 × 3%	200
(6 December 2015 to 5 April 2016)	
	1,200
Less interest paid	(1,000)
Taxable benefit	200

Task 4.13

	✓
True	
False	✓

There is a taxable benefit of the amount of the loan written-off, however small the loan. The £10,000 limit only applies to the interest benefit.

BPP
LEARNING MEDIA

Task 4.14

(1) The taxable benefit for 2015/16 is:

> £ | 650

During 2015/16 Vimal will have a taxable benefit arising from the use of the asset:

£1,000 × 20% × 9/12 = £150

He will also have a benefit when the asset is sold to him at an undervalue.

This will be the higher of the MV at the date of the 'gift', and the original market value minus benefits assessed so far, less his £100 contribution.

	£	£
Market value at date of gift		300
Original market value		1,000
Assessed re use:		
2013/14: £1,000 × 20% × 3/12	50	
2014/15: £1,000 × 20%	200	
2015/16: £1,000 × 20% × 9/12	150	
		(400)
		600
ie Higher value used		600
Less Vimal's contribution		(100)
		500
His total benefit (for both use and 'gift') in 2015/16 will therefore be		650

(2) The taxable benefit for 2015/16 is:

> £ | 4,350

The taxable benefit for use of the flat is calculated as follows:

	£
Annual value	3,000
£(120,000 − 75,000) × 3% (expensive accommodation)	1,350
Taxable benefit	4,350

The original cost is used, not the value now.

Task 4.15

The total taxable benefits for 2015/16 are:

> £ | 625

	£
Medical insurance (cost to employer)	385
Childcare (exempt − £55 per week for a basic rate taxpayer)	0
Newspaper allowance (12 × £20)	240
Taxable benefits	625

Task 4.16

(1) The taxable benefit arising in respect of the accommodation provided for Rita in 2015/16 and purchase of the furniture is:

£	21,200

	£
Annual value (higher than rent paid)	4,000
Electricity	700
Gas	1,200
Water	500
Council tax	1,300
Repairs	3,500
Furniture (20% × £30,000 × 6/12)	3,000
Purchase of furniture (W)	7,000
	21,200

Working

Purchase of furniture

Benefit is the **higher** of:

		£
(a)	Cost	30,000
	Less taxed for use of furniture (20% × £30,000 × 6/12)	(3,000)
		27,000
	Less amount paid by Rita	(20,000)
		7,000
(b)	Market value	25,000
	Less amount paid	(20,000)
		5,000

(2) The taxable benefit arising in respect of the relocation expenses is:

£	4,000

£12,000 – £8,000

(3) The taxable benefit arising in respect of the interest free loan in 2015/16 is:

£	Nil

No taxable benefit arises if the combined outstanding balance on all loans to the employee did not exceed £10,000 at any time in the tax year.

Task 4.17

	✓
£800	
£1,460	
£260	✓
£660	

	£
Annual value	800
Less contribution (£100 × 12 = £1,200)	(800)
	Nil

Additional charge

	£	£
Cost	97,000	
Less	(75,000)	
Excess	22,000	
£22,000 × 3%		660
Less contribution (£1,200 – £800)		(400)
Total benefit 2015/16		260

Task 4.18

	✓
Taxable benefit of £700	
Allowable expense of £700	✓
Allowable expense of £1,300	
Taxable benefit of £4,550	

	£	£
Amount received 13,000 × 35p		4,550
Less statutory amounts		
10,000 × 45p	4,500	
3,000 × 25p	750	
		(5,250)
Allowable expense		(700)

Task 4.19

Item	Taxable	Exempt
Interest on loan of £2,000 (only loan provided)		✓
Removal costs of £6,000		✓
Use of pool car		✓
Reimbursement of business expenses under a dispensation		✓
One staff party costing £100 per head		✓
Accommodation provided to employee who is not required to live in it for the performance of employment	✓	
Provision of parking space at work		✓
Additional costs of home-working of £4 per week		✓
Long service award of £800 for 22 years service		✓
Accommodation provided to a caretaker for proper performance of his employment duties		✓
Work related training		✓
Provision of second mobile phone	✓	

Task 4.20

	£
Salary	30,000
Less allowable expenses:	
reimbursed expenses	0
pension contribution (£30,000 × 8%)	(2,400)
professional body membership	(150)
fitness club membership	0
charitable donation (£50 × 12)	(600)
clothing	0
Employment income 2015/16	26,850

Task 4.21

The maximum amount of relocation expenses that his employer can pay without a taxable benefit arising is:

£	8,000

Task 4.22

	✓
£3,600	
£20,000	✓
£26,300	
£27,000	

The maximum contribution is the higher of £3,600 and his earnings of £20,000.

Dividends are not earnings.

Task 4.23

Zara's qualifying travel expenses for 2015/16 are:

£	2,100

£300 + £1,800. Travel expenses from home to a permanent workplace are not allowable.

Task 4.24

	✓
The employer deducts the contribution after calculating income tax under PAYE.	
The employer deducts basic rate tax from the contribution and the employee gets higher rate relief by extending the basic rate band in the tax computation.	
The employer deducts the contribution before calculating income tax under PAYE.	✓
The employer deducts basic rate tax from the contribution and there is no higher rate tax relief.	

The employer deducts the contribution before calculating income tax, so giving tax relief at the applicable rate/s.

Task 4.25

	✓
The pension contribution is paid net of basic rate tax, and higher rate tax relief is obtained by extending the basic rate band.	
The contribution is deducted from employment income as an allowable expense before tax is calculated under PAYE.	✓

Task 4.26

From:	AATStudent@boxmail.net
To:	MartinWilkes@boxmail.net
Sent:	14 March 2016 12:29
Subject:	Car

The car benefit is a percentage of the car's list price, not the actual price paid by the employer.

The percentage (that is multiplied by the list price) is dependant on the car's CO_2 emissions rating. For cars which emit CO_2 of 95g/km or more the percentage is 14%, however this percentage increases by 1% for every additional whole 5g/km of CO_2 emissions above 95g/km, up to a maximum of 35%.

In this case, the percentage would be 14% + 15% = 29%.

The percentage is further increased by 3% for a diesel car – has this car got a petrol or a diesel engine?

As the employer will be paying for fuel used for private motoring, a fuel benefit arises. The benefit is a percentage of £22,100. The percentage is the same percentage as is used to calculate the car benefit.

No benefit arises if you reimburse the whole of the expense of any fuel provided for private use, but there is **no** reduction to the benefit if only part of the expense for private use fuel is reimbursed, as here. It would be better for the contribution to be set against the use of the car, as this would be deductible in calculating the car benefit.

Task 4.27

Name	Jill Gilks
Box 1	60000.00
Box 2	13900.00
Box 5	Beata plc
Box 9	5200.00
Box 10	2000.00
Box 16	2250.00
Box 17	2250.00
Box 19	225.00

Answer bank

Chapter 5

Task 5.1

Simran's property income for 2015/16 is:

	✓
£2,080	
£1,990	
£2,040	
£2,130	✓

	£
Rent received (9 months × £500 – accruals basis)	4,500
Less electricity	(1,200)
water rates	(500)
insurance 9/12 × £360	(270)
wear and tear £(4,500 – 500) × 10%	(400)
Property income 2015/16	2,130

Task 5.2

What amount of taxable property income does Julie have for 2015/16?

£	3,120

	£
Rent received (£6,300 × 8/12)	4,200
Less expenses	(660)
Wear and tear (£4,200 × 10%)	(420)
Property income 2015/16	3,120

Room in own house

Exempt under rent a room (gross rent less than £4,250)

Task 5.3

Zelda's property income for 2015/16 is:

£	4,500

2013/14	£
Income	6,000
Expenses	(10,000)
Loss cfwd	(4,000)

2014/15	
Income	8,000
Expenses	(5,500)
	2,500
Less loss b/f	(2,500)
	Nil

Loss cfwd £1,500 (£4,000 - £2,500)

2015/16	
Income	10,000
Expenses	(4,000)
	6,000
Less loss b/f	(1,500)
Taxable property income 2015/16	4,500

Task 5.4

Nitin's property income for 2015/16 is:

£	4,154

	£
Rent (£3,600 × 3)	10,800
Rent (£4,000 × 1)	4,000
	14,800
Less water rates	(195)
insurance (£480 × 6/12)	(240)
interest (£350,000 × 5% × 6/12)	(8,750)
initial repairs: capital	0
Wear and tear allowance £(14,800 − 195) × 10%	(1,461)
Property income 2015/16	4,154

Task 5.5

Sinead's property income for 2015/16 is:

£	4,600

	£
Property one: rent (9/12 × £8,000)	6,000
Property two: rent (4 × £450)	1,800
Less expenses on property one	(1,200)
expenses on property two	(2,000)
Property income 2015/16	4,600

Task 5.6

Suzy's property income for 2015/16 is:

£	1,750

	£
Property income (12 × £500)	6,000
Less expenses on property	(3,700)
	2,300

	£
Property income (12 × £500)	6,000
Less rent a room relief	(4,250)
Property income 2015/16	1,750

Suzy will elect for rent a room relief as this gives a lower assessable amount.

Task 5.7

	✓
Setting the loss of £(5,000) against her employment income in 2015/15	
Carrying forward the loss of £(5,000) against property income in 2016/17	
Setting the loss of £(5,000) first against the profit of £3,000 in 2015/16 and then carrying forward the balance of £(2,000) against property income in 2016/17	✓
Setting the loss of £(5,000) first against the profit of £3,000 in 2015/16 and then setting the balance of £(2,000) against employment income in 2015/16	

Task 5.8

A property can qualify as qualifying holiday accommodation if it is:

Available for letting to the public as holiday accommodation for at least | 210 |
days in the tax year and actually let for at least | 105 | days during the same tax
year and not normally occupied for periods of 'longer term occupation' (more than 31
consecutive days to the same person) for more than | 155 | days in a tax year.

Task 5.9

	✓
True	
False	✓

Losses on qualifying holiday accommodation cannot be set against other income, or
property income that doesn't qualify as holiday accommodation. Losses from qualifying
holiday accommodation can only be set against income from the same holiday letting
business.

Task 5.10

	✓
True	
False	✓

To be qualifying holiday accommodation, the property must be situated in the EEA (which
includes the UK).

Task 5.11

Olivia's property income loss for 2015/16 is:

£	(420)

	£
Property income (52 × £40)	2,080
Less expenses on property	(2,500)
Property income loss	(420)

Olivia will elect to set aside rent a room relief in order to give herself a property loss. Otherwise as her gross rental income does not exceed £4,250, rent a room relief would apply automatically and the income and expenses would be ignored for tax purposes.

Task 5.12

	✓
The income qualifies as earnings for pension purposes	
The wear and tear allowance applies	✓
Capital allowances are available on furniture	

The wear and tear allowance is not available in relation to furnished holiday property. Landlords of qualifying holiday accommodation can claim capital allowances on furniture instead.

Task 5.13

The property income taxable on Len for 2015/16 assuming that he uses the rent a room scheme is:

	✓
£90	
£430	✓
£4,316	
£4,680	

	£
Income from letting (£90 × 52)	4,680
Less rent a room relief	(4,250)
Taxable property income	430

Task 5.14

> **Qualifying holiday accommodation**
>
> For a property to be qualifying holiday accommodation, the property must, broadly, be:
>
> (a) Furnished accommodation
>
> (b) Situated in the European Economic Area
>
> (c) Let on commercial basis with a view to realisation of profit
>
> (d) Available for commercial letting to the public for not less than 210 days in a tax year
>
> (e) Actually let for not less than 105 days within the 210 day period
>
> (f) Not more than 155 days of the tax year must fall during periods of longer term occupation. Longer term occupation is described as a continuous period of more than 31 days during which the accommodation is in the same occupation.
>
> The income tax advantages are:
>
> (a) The income qualifies as earnings for pension purposes.
>
> (b) Capital allowances are available on furniture. The wear and tear allowance does not apply.

Task 5.15

Page 1
Your name   Pierce Jones
Box 1   1

Page 2
Box 20   6000.00 (£500 x 12)
Box 24   650.00 (£400 + £250)
Box 26   3200.00
Box 29   1200.00
Box 38   950.00
Box 40   950.00

Chapter 6

Task 6.1

By which date should an individual normally submit his 2015/16 self assessment tax return if it is to be filed online?

	✓
31 January 2017	✓
5 April 2017	
31 October 2016	
31 December 2016	

Task 6.2

How will Gordon settle his income tax payable for 2015/16?

	✓
The full amount of £17,000 will be paid on 31 January 2017	
Payments on account of £7,250 will be made on 31 January and 31 July 2016, with nothing due on 31 January 2017	
Payments on account of £8,500 will be made on 31 January and 31 July 2016 with nothing due on 31 January 2017	
Payments on account of £7,250 will be made on 31 January and 31 July 2016, with the balance of £2,500 being paid on 31 January 2017	✓

Task 6.3

What is the latest date until which Pat must retain records of his income?

	✓
All records until 31 January 2018	
Property income until 31 January 2018, dividend income until 31 January 2022	
Property income until 31 January 2022, dividend income until 31 January 2018	
All records until 31 January 2022	✓

Task 6.4

The minimum penalty as a percentage of Potential Lost Revenue for a deliberate but not concealed error on a tax return, for which is there is an unprompted disclosure is:

	✓
0%	
20%	✓
30%	
35%	

Task 6.5

The maximum penalty per tax year for failing to keep records is:

£ | 3,000

Task 6.6

Dear John

Income tax return

I am writing to let you know that I will need the following information and documents in order to complete your income tax return for the year to 5 April 2016:

(1) **Forms P60 and P11D**

Both of these forms should have been supplied to you by your employer. Form P60 will give me details of your salary and tax deducted from it. Form P11D will give me the details I need regarding your company car and private medical insurance.

(2) **Bank and Building Society Certificates of annual interest earned**

These will provide the details I need regarding your taxable interest and the tax deducted from it.

(3) **Annual pension statement**

This will give me the details I need of your pension payments and of any tax withheld at source from the payments.

(4) **Receipted subscription notice**

This will show me details of the subscription you have paid.

I do not need any details of either your mortgage payments or of the interest arising on your ISA account. This is because there is no tax relief for mortgage payments, and the interest arising on your ISA account is tax-free.

(a) Your completed tax return must be submitted to HMRC by 31 January 2017 providing you submit it online. If you want to file a paper return, you would need to submit it by 31 October 2016.

(b) Any outstanding tax is due for payment on 31 January 2017.

(c) A fixed penalty of £100 applies if your tax return is not submitted online by 31 January 2017. In addition, if the return is more than three months late, then a potential daily penalty of £10 per day may be imposed from then on and this can apply for up to 90 days. There is a further penalty of 5% of tax due if the return is more than six months late (minimum of £300). Another further penalty is charged if the return is more than 12 months late. This is 5% of tax due (minimum £300) unless the withholding of information is deliberate and concealed or deliberate but not concealed when it rises to 100% or 70% respectively.

Interest is charged on a daily basis in respect of any tax paid late. There is a penalty of 5% of tax due 30 days after the due date. A further 5% penalty is charged where the tax is still unpaid at six and twelve months after the due date. This gives a maximum penalty of 15% of the unpaid tax.

(d) Finally, in response to the final point in your letter, a husband and wife are taxed independently, so there will be no need for us to consider your wife's income when completing your tax return.

Yours sincerely

Peter Jones

Task 6.7

From:	AATStudent@boxmail.net
To:	Dicer@hotnet.net
Sent:	1 December 2016
Subject:	Information

First, as I have submitted the tax return, we need to notify HM Revenue & Customs as soon as possible that there are omissions. However, there should be no penalties, as there should be no additional tax due. I will explain why this is the case.

On the tax return, we need to declare your gross income, which will include all sources of income, even those from which tax has already been deducted. The total tax liability is then calculated, and the tax you have already paid is deducted.

In your case, as you are not a higher or additional rate taxpayer, there will be no additional tax to pay.

For the building society interest, we need to gross it up by the 20% tax already deducted, and declare £190 (being £152 x 100/80). The income tax due on this will have been deducted by the building society before paying you the interest, and so there is no further tax to pay.

The interest from the ISA is exempt from tax, so there is no need to declare that income.

The Gift Aid donation that you paid to the National Trust would get additional tax relief if you paid tax at the higher or additional rate, but as you do not, there will be no effect.

I will inform HMRC as soon as possible on your behalf, but there should be no penalties to pay.

Task 6.8

From:	AATStudent@boxmail.net
To:	clarissa@hotnet.net
Sent:	17 September 2016
Subject:	Worried

The maximum penalty for a careless (rather than a deliberate) error is 30% of the potential lost revenue (ie tax lost). The potential lost revenue here is £420 × 20% = £84 so the maximum penalty is £25.20.

However, this may be reduced to 0% if you disclose the error to HMRC when you have no reason to believe HMRC has discovered, or is about to discover, the error. You should therefore make disclosure to HMRC as soon as possible.

Interest is payable on the £84 tax due. This will be charged from 31 January 2016 to the day before it is paid so again you should make sure that you pay it as soon as possible.

Task 6.9

The usual rules are that half of the tax liability for any year is paid by 31 January in that tax year and the other half is paid by 31 July following the tax year.

This is based on an estimate, using the preceding tax year's tax payable figure and the payments are called payments on account. A balancing payment is made on 31 January following the tax year, if required, or a repayment made by HMRC if the tax payable is less than the total of the payments on account.

Since 2015/16 was the first tax year in which you had property income, there were no payments on account and you just pay the whole liability by 31 January 2017.

However for 2016/17 you are required to make payments on account. This is based on the tax payable for 2015/16 which is why the payment required on 31 January 2017 for 2016/17 is half of £5,000, that is £2,500.

If you overpay for 2016/17, you will receive a refund from HMRC.

You can claim to reduce these payments on account as you think that your property income will not be as high as it was last year. You need to estimate what your property income will be for 2016/17, the tax that will be payable on it and then apply to reduce the payments on account to half of this amount.

But you do need to be careful because if you make an incorrect claim to reduce these payments on account, then HMRC will charge you interest on the difference between what should have been paid and what was actually paid and may also charge you a penalty if the claim was made negligently.

Chapter 7

Task 7.1

For the gain on the disposal of a capital asset to be a chargeable gain there must be a chargeable

disposal

of a chargeable

asset

by a chargeable

person

Task 7.2

Item	Chargeable asset	Exempt asset
Car		✓
A plot of land	✓	
Jewellery	✓	
Premium bonds		✓
Government stock ('gilts')		✓

Task 7.3

	✓
The gift of an asset	
The sale of part of an asset	
The transfer of an asset on death	✓
The sale of the whole of an asset	

Task 7.4

	✓
£34,000	✓
£39,000	
£45,000	
£50,000	

	£
Proceeds of sale	90,100
Less cost	(40,000)
Less enhancement expenditure	(5,000)
Chargeable gain	45,100
Less annual exempt amount	(11,100)
Taxable gain	34,000

Task 7.5

(1) Lenny's capital gains tax liability for 2015/16 is:

£ 1,523

	£
Chargeable gains	20,100
Less allowable losses	(3,560)
Net chargeable gains	16,540
Less annual exempt amount	(11,100)
Taxable gains	5,440
CGT: £5,440 × 28%	1,523

(2) Lenny's capital gains tax liability is payable by:

31/01/2017

Task 7.6

Larry's capital gains tax liability for 2015/16 is:

£	2,064

	£
Chargeable gains	25,100
Less allowable losses	(5,200)
Net chargeable gains	19,900
Less annual exempt amount	(11,100)
Taxable gains	8,800

CGT payable

	£
£4,000 × 18%	720
£4,800 × 28%	1,344
	2,064

....

Task 7.7

Laura's capital gains tax liability for 2015/16 is:

£	2,454

	£
Chargeable gains (£5,100 + £17,500)	22,600
Less allowable losses	(2,000)
Net chargeable gains	20,600
Less annual exempt amount	(11,100)
Taxable gains	9,500

CGT payable

	£
£2,065 (W) × 18%	372
£7,435 × 28%	2,082
	2,454

(W) Unused basic rate band is £31,785 – £29,720 = £2,065

....

Task 7.8

Lisa's capital gains tax liability for 2015/16 is:

£	3,884

	£
Chargeable gains	27,100
Less annual exempt amount	(11,100)
Taxable gains	16,000

CGT

£5,965 (W) × 18%	1,074
£10,035 × 28%	2,810
	3,884

(W) Unused basic rate band is £31,785 – £25,820 = £5,965

Task 7.9

(1) The cost of the land sold is:

£	120,000

$$\frac{240,000}{240,000+60,000} \times £150,000$$

(2) The chargeable gain on sale is:

£	117,000

	£
Disposal proceeds	240,000
Less disposal costs	(3,000)
Net proceeds	237,000
Less cost	(120,000)
Chargeable gain	117,000

Task 7.10

	✓
The full amount will be paid on 31 January 2017	✓
The full amount will be paid on 31 January 2016	
Payments on account will be made on 31 January and 31 July 2016, with the balance being paid on 31 January 2017	
Payments on account will be made on 31 January and 31 July 2015, with the balance being paid on 31 January 2016	

Task 7.11

The losses to carry forward to 2016/17 are:

£ | 4,900

	£
Gains	18,200
Losses	(7,000)
	11,200
Losses b/f £(11,200 – 11,100)	(100)
	11,100
Less annual exempt amount	(11,100)
Taxable gains	Nil

Losses c/f £(5,000 – 100) = £4,900

Task 7.12

Mike's chargeable gain on sale is:

£ | 7,000

	£
Proceeds of sale	16,000
Less allowable cost (value at death)	(9,000)
Chargeable gain	7,000

Task 7.13

Luke's chargeable gain on sale is:

£	17,000

	£
Proceeds of sale	25,000
Less disposal costs	(2,500)
Net proceeds of sale	22,500
Less allowable cost	
25,000/(25,000 + 50,000) × £(15,000 + 1,500)	(5,500)
Chargeable gain	17,000

Task 7.14

	✓
True	✓
False	

If an individual has allowable losses brought forward, these are only used to bring gains down to the annual exempt amount.

Task 7.15

The maximum allowable loss carried forward to 2016/17 will be:

£	11,700

Tax year	2013/14	2014/15	2015/16
	£	£	£
Gains	2,000	4,000	13,400
Losses	(14,000)	(2,000)	(2,000)
Net gain/(loss)	(12,000)	2,000	11,400
Less loss b/f	(0)	0	(300)
Less annual exempt amount	0	(2,000)	(11,100)
Chargeable gain	0	0	0
Loss c/f	(12,000)	(12,000)	(11,700)

The use of the loss brought forward in 2015/16 is restricted to leave chargeable gains equal to the annual exempt amount.

Task 7.16

	✓
Mike	
Susan	
Simon	
Sarah	✓

Mary is connected to her spouse (Mike), her sister-in-law (Susan) and her brother-in-law (Simon). Mary is not connected to her niece (Sarah).

Task 7.17

The loss of £(3,000) can be set against the gain of £5,000.

	✓
True	
False	✓

The loss of £(3,000) can only be set against gains on disposals made to the son (ie the same connected person) in the same tax year or future tax years.

Task 7.18

Her chargeable gain on sale is:

£	833

	£
Gross proceeds	6,500
Less costs of sale	(130)
Net proceeds	6,370
Less cost	(1,500)
Chargeable gain	4,870
Gain cannot exceed 5/3 × £(6,500 − 6,000)	833

Task 7.19

Jolyon's allowable loss is:

£	1,125

	£
Deemed proceeds	6,000
Less costs of sale	(125)
Net proceeds	5,875
Less cost	(7,000)
Allowable loss	(1,125)

Task 7.20

Rowenna has a chargeable gain on sale of £1,500.

	✓
True	
False	✓

Both the proceeds and the cost are less than £6,000 so the gain is exempt.

Task 7.21

Her chargeable gain on sale is:

	✓
£1,200	
£2,000	
£2,500	✓
£3,700	

	£
Gross proceeds	7,500
Less costs of sale	(300)
Net proceeds	7,200
Less cost	(3,500)
Chargeable gain	3,700
Gain cannot exceed 5/3 × £(7,500 – 6,000)	2,500

··

Task 7.22

Mark's allowable loss is:

£	(3,500)

	£
Deemed proceeds	6,000
Less costs of sale	(500)
Net proceeds	5,500
Less cost	(9,000)
Allowable loss	(3,500)

··

Task 7.23

Box 1	Isabel Redding
Box 3	19100.00
Box 6	2500.00
Box 7	1750.00
Box 18	1
Box 19	7000.00
Box 20	9500.00
Box 21	0
Box 24	1
Box 25	5000.00
Box 26	2800.00
Box 27	2200.00
Box 30	1
Box 31	30000.00
Box 32	13100.00
Box 33	16900.00

Chapter 8

Task 8.1

	✓
Against 10,000 of the shares purchased on 10 May 2008	
Against 5,000 of the shares purchased on 24 January 2016 and then against 5,000 of the shares purchased on 10 May 2008	
Against 10,000 of the total shareholding of 20,000 shares	
Against the 8,000 shares purchased on 24 January 2016 and then against 2,000 of the shares purchased on 10 May 2008	✓

Task 8.2

His net chargeable gain on sale is:

£	9,800

Mr Stevens will match his disposal of 5,000 shares on 10 August 2015 to acquisitions as follows:

1. 1,000 shares bought on 16 August 2015 (next 30 days, FIFO basis)

2. 4,000 shares from the share pool (which only consists of the 6,000 shares bought in July 2014)

Disposal of 1,000 shares bought on 16 August 2015

	£
Proceeds of sale £20,000 × 1,000/5,000	4,000
Less cost	(4,200)
Allowable loss	(200)

Disposal of 4,000 shares bought from the share pool (= July 2014 acquisition)

	£
Proceeds of sale £20,000 × 4,000/5,000	16,000
Less cost £9,000 × 4,000/6,000	(6,000)
Chargeable gain	10,000
Net chargeable gain = £10,000 – 200	9,800

Task 8.3

Share pool

	No. of shares	Cost £
10 February 2001	12,000	18,000
20 September 2008 Bonus 1:4 (1/4 × 12,000 = 3,000 shares)	3,000	0
	15,000	18,000
15 March 2016 Disposal (£18,000 × 2,000/15,000 = £2,400)	(2,000)	(2,400)
	13,000	15,600

Gain on sale

	£
Proceeds	8,000
Less cost	(2,400)
Gain	5,600

Task 8.4

Mark will match his disposal of 10,000 shares on 4 November 2015 as follows:

1. 2,000 shares bought on 10 November 2015
2. 8,000 shares from share pool

	£
Disposal of 2,000 shares bought on 10 November 2015	
Proceeds $\frac{2,000}{10,000} \times £60,000$	12,000
Less cost	(11,500)
Chargeable gain	500
Disposal of 8,000 shares from share pool	
Proceeds $\frac{8,000}{10,000} \times £60,000$	48,000
Less cost (W)	(12,200)
Chargeable gain	35,800
Total chargeable gain (£500 + £35,800)	36,300

Share pool working	*No. of shares*	*Cost* £
9 December 2001	12,000	4,400
12 October 2005 Rights 1:3 × £5	4,000	20,000
(1/3 × 12,000 = 4,000 shares × £5 = £20,000)		
	16,000	24,400
4 November 2015 Disposal	(8,000)	(12,200)
(£24,400 × 8,000/16,000 = £12,200)		
	8,000	12,200

Answer bank

Chapter 9

Task 9.1

	✓
16.5/25	✓
8.5/25	
15.5/25	
11.5/25	

	Chargeable	Exempt
Actual occupation		8
Employment abroad (actual occupation before and after period of absence) – any period		5
Actual occupation		2
Absence (not followed by period of actual occupation)	8.5	
Last 18 months of ownership		1.5
Totals	8.5	16.5

Task 9.2

	£
Proceeds	180,000
Less cost	(50,000)
Gain before PPR exemption	130,000
Less PPR exemption (£130,000 × 10/18)	(72,222)
Chargeable gain	57,778

Working

	Exempt years	Chargeable years
1.8.97 – 31.7.00 (actual occupation)	3	
1.8.00 – 31.7.04 (up to 4 years due to place of work not employed abroad)	4	
1.8.04 – 31.7.05 (up to 3 years any reason)	1	
1.8.05 – 31.1.06 (actual occupation)	½	
1.2.06 – 31.1.14 (not followed by actual occupation)		8
1.2.14 – 31.7.15 (last 1½ years)	1½	
Totals	10	8

AAT AQ2013
SAMPLE ASSESSMENT
PERSONAL TAX

Time allowed: 2 hours

Note that this AAT Sample Assessment FA15 is an updated version of the original FA14 Sample Assessment. It has been updated by the AAT on their website and in the BPP Question Bank independently so the version on the AAT website may not be identical to the version in this BPP book.

Taxation tables for personal tax – 2015/16

Taxation Data 1

Pop-up 1

Tax rates and bands

	%	£
Basic rate	20	first 31,785
Higher rate	40	to 150,000
Additional rate	45	over 150,000

Savings income is taxed at 0%, 20%, 40% and 45%.

(0% applies to a maximum of £5,000 of savings income only where non-savings income is below this limit)

Dividends are taxed at 10%, 32.5% and 37.5%.

Personal allowances

	£
Personal allowance for individuals born after 5 April 1948	10,600
Age allowance for individuals born before 6 April 1938	10,660
Income limit for age allowance	27,700

Taxation Data 2

Pop-up 2

Car benefit percentage

Emission rating for petrol engines	%
0g/km to 50g/km	5
51g/km to 75g/km	9
76g/km to 94g/km	13
95g/km or more	14 + 1% for every extra 5g/km above 95g/km

Diesel engines – additional 3%

The figure for fuel is £22,100

Authorised mileage rates

First 10,000 miles 45p
Over 10,000 miles 25p

Van scale charge

	£
Charge	3,150
Private fuel provided	594
Low emission van charge	630
HMRC official rate	3%

Capital gains tax

Annual exempt amount (annual exemption)	£11,100
Tax rate	18%
Higher rate	28%

Task 1 (9 marks)

George had the use of two company cars during 2015/16. The company paid for all the running costs of the cars, including all fuel.

Details of the cars are as follows:

	Periods of use	List price £	Cost £	CO₂ emission	Type of engine
Nissan	4 months of the tax year	18,500	17,800	139g/km	Petrol
Volvo	8 months of the tax year	22,800	20,300	167g/km	Diesel

Complete the following table to show George's taxable benefit in kind for the cars for 2015/16. Show monetary answers in whole pounds.

Car		%	£
Nissan	Scale charge percentage		
	Taxable benefit on provision of the car		
	Taxable benefit on provision of fuel		
Volvo	Scale charge percentage		
	Taxable benefit on provision of the car		
	Taxable benefit on provision of fuel		
Total taxable benefit			

Task 2 (10 marks)

(a) Indicate whether each of the following will or will not result in an assessable benefit in kind for the employee by dragging the correct item into the answer column of the table.

The following are provided by the employer to the employee	Answer
Free parking spaces outside the place of work.	
Provision of a £11,000 interest free loan.	
Contribution of £150 per year towards employee's household costs as the employee works from home one day per week.	
Free meals provided to all directors and senior managers.	

Drag items

Will be treated as an assessable benefit

Will **not** be treated as an assessable benefit

Roweena received the following benefits during 2015/16:

1. She was provided with the use of a house that was bought by her employer in March 2010 for £214,000. The house was extended and improved in October 2011 at a cost of £18,500. In June 2015, the house was further extended at a cost of £5,400. The house has an annual value of £4,700.

2. The furniture for the house was provided by her employer at a cost of £22,000.

3. On 1 November 2013, Roweena had been given a £15,000 loan on which she paid her employer 1% interest. On 1 July 2015, Roweena repaid £3,000 of the loan, but she had made no other repayments. No elections have been made in respect of the loan.

(b) **Complete the sentences below using this information.**

The cost of accommodation that will be used in the benefit in kind computation will be:

£ [   ]

The taxable benefit in kind arising from the accommodation will be:

£ [   ]

The taxable benefit in kind arising from the provision of the furniture will be:

£ [   ]

The taxable benefit in kind arising from the loan will be:

£ [   ]

BPP
LEARNING MEDIA

Task 3 (10 marks)

Barrie has a furnished house which he lets for £515 per calendar month.

His expenditure for the year was as follows:

Cost of redecoration	£1,000
Annual insurance premium from 1 January 2015	£1,800
Annual insurance premium from 1 January 2016	£2,200
Water rates	£600
Council tax	£2,150

(a) Calculate the profit or loss made on the property by inputting the correct figures in the boxes. Do not use brackets or minus signs and if you feel any items are not allowable please insert a zero '0'.

	£
Property income	
Property expenses:	
Redecoration	
Insurance	
Water rates	
Council tax	
Wear and tear	
PROFIT	

Charlene's only income is derived from the letting of property. She has profits and losses for the last few years as shown in the table below.

(b) Show how the loss made in 2014/15 would be relieved by selecting the appropriate figure from each of the drop-down lists. If you consider there to be no loss relieved in that year select the zero figure from the drop-down list.

	2013/14 £	2014/15 £	2015/16 £
Property income/(loss)	8,700	(2,200)	1,300
Loss relieved	[▼]	———	[▼]

Drop-down list:

0
(1,300)
(2,200)
(8,700)

Task 4 (6 marks)

Angela receives interest from an ISA, interest from a Building Society account and dividends from shares. Her other income, net of personal allowances, totalled £29,715 for 2015/16. She has no other sources of income.

Calculate the tax deducted at source and any additional tax payable for each type of income shown in the table below. If your answer is zero, please input a '0'. Your answer should be in pounds and pence.

Income	Income received £	Tax deducted at source £	Additional tax payable £
Interest from ISA	412		
Interest from Building Society	856		
Dividends	1,314		

Task 5 (12 marks)

Kayla, who was born in September 1967, provides you with the following information that relates to her income for 2015/16:

1) Her annual salary from 1 January 2015 was £105,800. On 1 January 2016 she received a 2% pay rise.

2) She has the use of a company car, on which the benefit in kind has been computed at £3,350. The company pays for all running costs, including the fuel and this benefit in kind has been computed at £4,190.

3) She paid an annual subscription to her professional body costing £290.

4) Kayla is in the company pension scheme. She pays 6% of her salary into this scheme, and her employer pays 8% of her salary.

5) During 2015/16, Kayla received £1,080 in interest from a building society account and £380 in interest from an ISA.

Complete the following table showing the figure that may be included in Kayla's taxable income for 2015/16. You should use whole pounds only. If your answer is zero, please input a '0'. Do not use brackets or minus signs.

	£
Salary	
Employee's pension contribution	
Employer's pension contribution	
Benefit in kind for cars	
Benefit in kind for fuel	
Professional subscription	
Interest from Building Society	
Interest from ISA	
Personal allowance	
Taxable Income	

Task 6 (10 marks)

Yubin, who is 36, has the following income for 2015/16:

	£
Total employment income	40,300
Interest received from Building Societies	1,480
Dividends received	774

(a) Calculate his total income tax liability for 2015/16, entering your answer and workings into the blank table below. You have been given more space than you will need.

Yubin is considering contributing into a private pension scheme, paying 5% of his employment income each year. However, he does not understand the taxation implications of doing this.

(b) Explain to Yubin how he will get tax relief on such contributions, and tax implications if he had paid into this scheme during 2015/16.

Task 7 (10 marks)

Today is 14 April 2016.

A new client has written to you explaining his situation. He has been self-employed for many years, but the last tax return he filed with HMRC was for the tax year 2013/14, which he filed on 1 October 2015. He has not filed any further returns.

He is now very worried about penalties that he may be charged.

In the box below, respond to the client's query by explaining what penalties he may incur due to the late filing of his tax returns.

Task 8 (7 marks)

Jermaine rented out two properties during 2015/16. The summary information from these properties is:

Property	Rental Income £	Repairs £	Council Tax
P – unfurnished	8,900	2,600	1,910
R – furnished	10,700	1,200	2,370

Where possible, Jermaine claims the wear and tear allowance.

Jermaine pays 8% of rents received in management fees. He had property losses of £4,300 from 2014/15.

Complete the relevant parts of the following tax return by inputting information into the boxes provided.

Property income

Do not include furnished holiday lettings, Real Estate Investment Trust or Property Authorised Investment Funds dividends/distributions here.

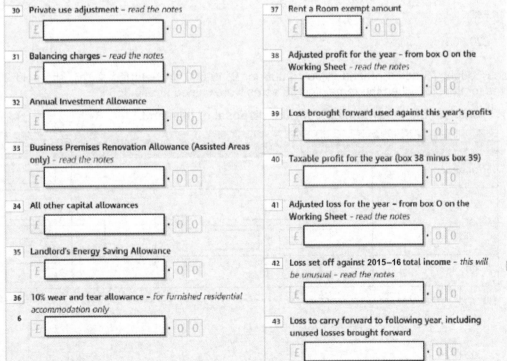

20 Total rents and other income from property

£ [   ] · 0 0

21 Tax taken off any income in box 20

£ [   ] · 0 0

22 Premiums for the grant of a lease – from box E on the Working Sheet – *read the notes*

£ [   ] · 0 0

23 Reverse premiums and inducements

£ [   ] · 0 0

Property expenses

24 Rent, rates, insurance, ground rents etc.

£ [   ] · 0 0

25 Property repairs, maintenance and renewals

£ [   ] · 0 0

26 Loan interest and other financial costs

£ [   ] · 0 0

27 Legal, management and other professional fees

£ [   ] · 0 0

28 Costs of services provided, including wages

£ [   ] · 0 0

29 Other allowable property expenses

£ [   ] · 0 0

Calculating your taxable profit or loss

30 Private use adjustment – *read the notes*

£ [   ] · 0 0

31 Balancing charges – *read the notes*

£ [   ] · 0 0

32 Annual Investment Allowance

£ [   ] · 0 0

33 Business Premises Renovation Allowance (Assisted Areas only) - *read the notes*

£ [   ] · 0 0

34 All other capital allowances

£ [   ] · 0 0

35 Landlord's Energy Saving Allowance

£ [   ] · 0 0

36 10% wear and tear allowance – *for furnished residential accommodation only*
6

£ [   ] · 0 0

37 Rent a Room exempt amount

£ [   ] · 0 0

38 Adjusted profit for the year – from box O on the Working Sheet - *read the notes*

£ [   ] · 0 0

39 Loss brought forward used against this year's profits

£ [   ] · 0 0

40 Taxable profit for the year (box 38 minus box 39)

£ [   ] · 0 0

41 Adjusted loss for the year – from box O on the Working Sheet - *read the notes*

£ [   ] · 0 0

42 Loss set off against 2015–16 total income – *this will be unusual - read the notes*

£ [   ] · 0 0

43 Loss to carry forward to following year, including unused losses brought forward

£ [   ] · 0 0

Task 9 (12 marks)

(a) Show whether the following statements are true or false.

	True	False
The destruction of a capital asset through fire would not be treated as a chargeable disposal for capital gains tax.	☐	☐
Disposals on the death of a taxpayer would be treated as exempt disposals for capital gains tax.	☐	☐
The sale of a racehorse would be treated as an exempt asset for the purposes of capital gains tax.	☐	☐
Wasting chattels are tangible movable items with an estimated life of fifty years or less.	☐	☐

Joyce bought an asset in April 2004 for £105,000, selling it in November 2015 for £148,600. Joyce paid auctioneer's commission of 7.5% when she bought the asset and auctioneer's fees of 10% on the sale value of the asset.

(b) Select the gain arising from the disposal of this asset from the list below.

£43,600 ☐

£35,725 ☐

£28,740 ☐

£20,865 ☐

Jules bought 75 acres of land in July 2006 for £112,500. In February 2016, she sold 20 acres for £85,200 when the remaining 35 acres were valued at £70,350.

(c) Complete the following table for the disposal of this land.

	Workings	£
Proceeds		☐
Cost	$\dfrac{\boxed{}}{\boxed{} + \boxed{}}$ × $\boxed{}$	☐
Gain		☐

Task 10 (8 marks)

Jason bought 1,950 shares in Landle Ltd in May 2003 for £46,800. In September 2005, there was a 1 for 10 bonus issue. In February 2007, he sold 700 shares for £19,600. On 12 November 2015, he sold 800 shares for £25,600. On 19 November 2015, he bought 400 shares for £12,000.

Clearly showing the balance of shares and their value to carry forward, calculate the gain made on the sale of the shares in 2015/16. All workings must be shown in your calculations.

Task 11 (6 marks)

Alex bought a house on 1 March 2003 for £178,000 and sold the property on 31 October 2015 for £312,000.

During the period of ownership the following occurred:

Period	
01.03.03-31.12.05	Alex lived in the property
01.01.06-31.06.07	Alex moved in with his sick brother
01.07.07-30.06.09	Alex lived in the property
01.07.09-31.12.12	Alex worked abroad
01.01.13-31.10.15	Alex lived in the property until he sold it

(a) **Input the correct answers in the boxes provided to complete the sentences. Where applicable round your answer to the nearest whole number.**

The total period of ownership of the house is [   ] months.

The period of Alex's actual and deemed residence is [   ] months.

The chargeable gain on the sale of the house is £ [   ].

The capital gains for three taxpayers for 2015/16 are shown in the table below, together with their capital losses brought forward from 2014/15. The gains are before deduction of the annual exempt amount.

(b) **Tick to show how much of each of the losses brought forward will be relieved in 2015/16.**

Taxpayer	Gain 2015/16	Loss 2014/15	Relieve all loss	Relieve some loss	Relieve no loss
Danny	£43,800	£35,900	☐	☐	☐
Daniel	£15,800	£3,900	☐	☐	☐
Danielle	£9,900	£4,400	☐	☐	☐

AAT AQ2013
SAMPLE ASSESSMENT
PERSONAL TAX

ANSWERS

Task 1 (9 marks)

Complete the following table to show George's taxable benefit in kind for the cars for 2015/16. Show your answer in pounds only.

Car		%	£
Nissan	Scale charge percentage	22	
	Taxable benefit on provision of the car		1,357
	Taxable benefit on provision of fuel		1,620
Volvo	Scale charge percentage	31	
	Taxable benefit on provision of the car		4,712
	Taxable benefit on provision of fuel		4,567
Total taxable benefit			12,256

Nissan

The CO_2 emissions of the car are 135g/km (rounded down to the nearest five below).

Amount over baseline figure 135 – 95 = 40g/km

Divide 40 by 5 = 8

The taxable percentage is 14% + 8% = 22%

Car benefit = £18,500 (list price) × 22% × 4/12

Fuel benefit = £22,100 × 22% × 4/12

Volvo

Scale charge percentage = 165g/km (rounded down) – 95 = 70g/km /5 = 14% + 14% + 3%

Car benefit = £22,800 (list price) × 31% × 8/12

Fuel benefit = £22,100 × 31% × 8/12

Task 2 (10 marks)

(a) Indicate whether each of the following will or will not result in an assessable benefit in kind for the employee by dragging the correct item into the answer column of the table.

The following are provided by the employer to the employee	Answer	Options
Free parking spaces outside the place of work.	Will **not** be treated as an assessable benefit in kind	Will be treated as an assessable benefit in kind
Provision of a £11,000 interest free loan.	Will be treated as an assessable benefit in kind	Will **not** be treated as an assessable benefit in kind
Contribution of £150 per year towards employee's household costs as the employee works from home one day per week.	Will **not** be treated as an assessable benefit in kind	
Free meals provided to all directors and senior managers.	Will be treated as an assessable benefit in kind	

(b) **Complete the sentences below using this information.**

The cost of accommodation that will be used in the benefit in kind computation will be
£ | 232,500 |

(cost plus improvements to beginning of current tax year)

The taxable benefit in kind arising from the accommodation will be £ | 9,425 |

(£4,700 + (£232,500 – £75,000) × 3%))

The taxable benefit in kind arising from the provision of the furniture will be
£ | 4,400 |

(£22,000 × 20%)

The taxable benefit in kind arising from the loan will be £ | 277 |

Interest at the official rate = (£15,000 + £12,000)/2 = £13,500 × 3% = £405

Less interest actually paid:

06/04/15 – 30/06/15 = 3 months

£15,000 × 1% × 3/12 = £38

01/07/15 – 05/04/16 = 9 months

£12,000 × 1% × 9/12 = £90

The taxable benefit in kind is therefore £405 – £(38 + 90) = £277

Tutorial note

The strict method produces a benefit in kind of

(£15,000 x 2% × 3/12) + (£12,000 × 2% × 9/12) = £255

Task 3 (10 marks)

(a) **Calculate the profit or loss made on the property by inputting the correct figures in the boxes. Do not use brackets or minus signs and if you feel any items are not allowable please insert a zero '0'.**

	£
Property income (£515 × 12)	6,180
Property expenses:	
Redecoration	1,000
Insurance (£1,800 × 9/12) + (£2,200 × 3/12)	1,900
Water rates	600
Council tax	2,150
Wear and tear (£6,180 – £600 – £2,150) × 10%	343
PROFIT	187

Charlene's only income is derived from the letting of property. She has profits and losses for the last few years as shown in the table below.

(b) **Show how the loss made in 2014/15 would be relieved by selecting the appropriate figure from each of the drop-down lists. If you consider there to be no loss relieved in that year select the zero figure from the drop-down list.**

	2013/14 £	2014/15 £	2015/16 £
Property income/(loss)	8,700	(2,200)	1,300
Loss relieved	0 ▼	–	(1,300) ▼

Task 4 (6 marks)

Angela receives interest from an ISA, interest from a Building Society account and dividends from shares. Her other income, net of personal allowances, totalled £29,715 for 2015/16. She has no other sources of income.

Calculate the tax deducted at source and any additional tax payable for each type of income shown in the table below. If your answer is zero, please input a '0'. Your answer should be in pounds and pence.

Income	Income received £	Tax deducted at source £	Additional tax payable £
Interest from ISA	412	0	0 (Exempt income)
Interest from Building Society	856	214 (£856 × 20/80)	0 (Gross income of £1,070 fall in basic rate band)
Dividends	1,314	146 (£1,314 × 10/90)	103.50 (Gross income = £1,460. £1,000 falls in basic rate band and £460 taxed at 22.5% (32.5 – 10))

Task 5 (12 marks)

Complete the following table showing the figure that may be included in Kayla's taxable income for 2015/16. You should use whole pounds only. If your answer is zero, please input a '0'. Do not use brackets or minus signs.

	£
Salary (£105,800 × 9/12) + (£105,800 × 102% × 3/12)	106,329
Employee's pension contribution (6% × £106,329)	6,380
Employers pension contribution (exempt benefit)	0
Benefit in kind for cars	3,350
Benefit in kind for fuel	4,190
Professional subscription	290
Interest from Building Society (£1,080 × 100/80)	1,350
Interest from ISA	0
Total income	108,549
Personal allowance £(10,600 − 4,274 (108,549 − 100,000)/2))	6,325
Taxable income	102,224

Task 6 (10 marks)

Yubin, who is 36, has the following income for 2015/16:

	£
Total employment income	40,300
Interest received from Building Societies	1,480
Dividends received	774

(a) **Calculate his total income tax liability for 2015/16, entering your answer and workings into the blank table below. You have been given more space than you will need.**

	Workings	£
Employment income		40,300
Building society interest	£1,480 × 100/80	1,850
Dividends	£774 × 100/90	860
		43,010
Personal allowance		10,600
		32,410
£29,700 × 20%	£(40,300 – 10,600)	5,940
£1,850 × 20%		370
£235 × 10%	£(31,785-29,700-1,850)	24
£625 × 32.5%	£(860 – 235)	203
Total		6,537

Yubin is considering contributing into a private pension scheme, paying 5% of his employment income each year. However, he does not understand the taxation implications of doing this.

(b) **Explain to Yubin how he will get tax relief on such contributions, and tax implications if he had paid into this scheme during 2015/16.**

If Yubin contributes 5% of his employment income into a personal pension scheme, this will total £2,015. This amount will be grossed up for the basic rate, giving a total of £2,519. This amount is then used to extend the basic rate of income tax, so that he would not pay the higher rate until his taxable income was £34,304 (31,785 + 2,519). This would therefore mean that all his income for 2015/16 would be taxable at the basic rate.

Task 7 (10 marks)

Today is 14 April 2016.

A new client has written to you explaining his situation. He has been self-employed for many years, but the last tax return he filed with HMRC was for the tax year 2013/14, which he filed on 1 October 2015. He has not filed any further returns.

He is now very worried about penalties that he may be charged.

In the box below you need to respond to the client's query by explaining what penalties he may incur due to late filing of his tax returns.

The 2013/14 tax return should have been filed by 31 January 2015. The client filed it 8 months late and so he will incur a penalty. This penalty may consist of: an immediate £100 fine; a daily penalty of £10 per day to a maximum of £900; penalty of £300 or 5% of the tax liability for the year.

The 2014/15 tax return was also due to be filed by 31 January 2016, so by 14th April, this is 2½ months late. An immediate fine of £100 will be due, but provided he files it before 30th April 2016, he should avoid further penalties.

Task 8 (7 marks)

Box 20: 19,600

Box 24: 4,280

Box 25: 3,800

Box 27: 1,568 (19,600 × 8%)

Box 36: 833 (10,700 – 2370 × 10%)

Box 38: 9,119

Box 39: 4,300

Box 40: 4,819

Task 9 (12 marks)

(a) **Show whether the following statements are true or false.**

	True	False
The destruction of a capital asset through fire would not be treated as a chargeable disposal for capital gains tax.	☐	✓
Disposals on the death of a taxpayer would be treated as exempt disposals for capital gains tax.	✓	☐
The sale of a racehorse would be treated as an exempt asset for the purposes of capital gains tax.	✓	☐
Wasting chattels are tangible movable items with an estimated life of fifty years or less.	✓	☐

Joyce bought an asset in April 2004 for £105,000, selling it in November 2015 for £148,600. Joyce paid auctioneers commission of 7.5% when she bought the asset and auctioneer's fees of 10% on the sale value of the asset.

(b) **Select the gain arising from the disposal of this asset from the list below.**

£43,600   ☐

£35,725   ☐

£28,740   ☐

£20,865   ✓

Proceeds	£148,600 – £14,860 =	£133,740
Less cost	£105,000 + £7,875 =	(£112,875)
Gain		£20,865

Jules bought 75 acres of land in July 2006 for £112,500. In February 2016, she sold 40 acres for £85,200 when the remaining 35 acres were valued at £70,350.

(c) **Complete the following table for the disposal of this land.**

	Workings £	£
Proceeds		85,200
Cost	$\dfrac{85,200}{85,200+70,350}\times112,500$	61,620
Gain		23,580

Note. Under the costs workings on the second line, the answer 85,200 + 70,360 may also be written in as 70,350 + 85,200

Task 10 (8 marks)

Jason bought 1,950 shares in Landle Ltd in May 2003 for £46,800. In September 2005, there was a 1 for 10 bonus issue. In February 2007, he sold 700 shares for £19,600. On 12 November 2015, he sold 800 shares for £25,600. On 19 November 2015, he bought 400 shares for £12,000.

Clearly showing the balance of shares and their value to carry forward, calculate the gain made on the sale of the shares in 2015/16. All workings must be shown in your calculations.

	Event	Shares	£
May 2003	Purchase	1,950	46,800
September 2005	Bonus issue	195	
		2,145	
February 2007	Disposal	(700)	(15,273)
		1,445	31,527
November 2015	Disposal	(400)	(8,727)
		1,045	22,800
		Next 30 days (400)	Share pool (400)
Proceeds	£25,600 × 400/800	12,800	12,800
Cost		12,000	8,727
		800	4,073
Total gain	£800 + £4,073		4,873

Task 11 (6 marks)

Alex bought a house on 1 March 2003 for £178,000 and sold the property on 31 October 2015 for £312,000.
During the period of ownership the following occurred:

Period	
01.03.03-31.12.05	Alex lived in the property
01.01.06-31.06.07	Alex moved in with his sick brother
01.07.07-30.06.09	Alex lived in the property
01.07.09-31.12.12	Alex worked abroad
01.01.13-31.10.15	Alex lived in the property until he sold it

(a) Input the correct answers in the boxes provided to complete the sentences. Where applicable round your answer to the nearest whole number.

The total period of ownership of the house is 152 months.

The period of Alex's actual and deemed residence 152 months.

The chargeable gain on the sale of the house is £ 0 .

The capital gains for three taxpayers for 2015/16 are shown in the table below, together with their capital losses brought forward from 2014/15. The gains are before deduction of the annual exempt amount.

(b) Tick to show how much of each of the losses brought forward will be relieved in 2015/16.

Taxpayer	Gain 2014/15	Loss 2013/14	Relieve all loss	Relieve some loss	Relieve no loss
Danny	£43,800	£35,900		✓	
Daniel	£15,800	£3,900	✓		
Danielle	£9,900	£4,400			✓

BPP PRACTICE ASSESSMENT 1
PERSONAL TAX

Time allowed: 2 hours

PRACTICE ASSESSMENT 1

TAXATION DATA

Taxation tables for personal tax – 2015/16

Note that 'TAXATION DATA 1' and 'TAXATION DATA 2' shown below will be available as pop-up windows throughout your live assessment.

TAXATION DATA 1

Pop-up 1

Tax rates and bands

	%	£
Basic rate	20	first 31,785
Higher rate	40	to 150,000
Additional rate	45	over 150,000

Savings income is taxed at 0%, 20%, 40% and 45%.

(0% applies to a maximum of £5,000 of savings income only where non-savings income is below this limit)

Dividends are taxed at 10%, 32.5% and 37.5%.

Personal allowances

	£
Personal allowance for individuals born after 5 April 1938	10,600
Age allowance for individuals born before 6 April 1938	10,660
Income limit for age allowance	27,700

TAXATION DATA 2

Pop-up 2

Car benefit percentage

Emission rating for petrol engines	%
0g/km to 50g/km	5
51g/km to 75g/km	9
76g/km to 94g/km	13
95g/km or more	14% + 1% for every extra 5g/km above 95g/km

Diesel engines – additional 3%

The figure for fuel is £22,100

Authorised mileage rates

First 10,000 miles	45p
Over 10,000 miles	25p

Van scale charge

	£
Charge	3,150
Private fuel provided	594
Low emission van charge	630

HMRC official rate

3%

Capital gains tax

Annual exempt amount	£11,100
Tax rate	18%
Higher rate	28%

Task 1

Shane is provided with a company car for business and private use throughout 2015/16. The car had a list price of £16,700 when bought new in December 2013, although the company paid £15,000 for the car after a dealer discount. It has a petrol engine, with CO_2 emissions of 144g/km. The company pays for all running costs, including all fuel. Shane does not make any contribution for his private use of the car.

(1) **The cost of the car in the taxable benefit computation is:**

£ *16 700*

(2) **The percentage used in the taxable benefit computation is:**

23 %

(3) **The taxable benefit in respect of the provision of fuel for private use is:**

£ *5083*

....

Task 2

(a) Josie is a basic rate taxpayer and receives the following benefits as the result of her employment.

In each case enter the taxable benefit arising in 2015/16. If the benefit is exempt, enter 0.

(1) A mobile telephone for private and business use throughout the year. The purchase of the phone and the calls from it cost her employer a total of £350 for 2015/16.

£ *0*

(2) Childcare vouchers of £100 per week for 48 weeks during 2015/16.

£ *2160*

(3) Leisure club membership for Josie costing £5,000 using a corporate discount scheme. If a member of the public had taken this membership it would have cost £6,500.

£ *5000*

(4) Use of a house near her work that enables her to start work at 7.00am every morning. The house has an annual value of £5,900 and cost her employer £227,000 4 years ago.

5900
4560

£ *10460*

(b) For each of the following benefits, tick whether they would be wholly or partly taxable or wholly exempt if received in 2015/16:

Item	Wholly or partly taxable	Wholly exempt
Interest on loan of £8,000 (only loan provided)		✓
Additional costs of home working of £5 per week (no evidence presented to employer)	✓	
Use of pool car		✓
One staff party costing £120 per head		✓

Task 3

(a) Emily lets a furnished house for £150 a week. During 2015/16 the flat was let for 40 weeks. It was unoccupied for the remaining 12 weeks of the year.

During 2015/16, Emily spent £190 on advertising for tenants, £460 on water rates, £800 on redecoration, £690 on electricity and £368 on cleaning. Emily also installed a new central heating system at a cost of £1,200. She claims the wear and tear allowance where possible.

Calculate the property income taxable on Emily for 2015/16 using the proforma layout provided. Fill in all the unshaded boxes. If any item is not an allowable expense, enter 0. Both brackets and minus signs can be used to show negative numbers.

	£
Rent	6000
Expenses:	
Advertising	(190)
Water rates	(460)
Redecoration	(800)
Electricity	(690)
Cleaning	(368)
Central heating system	0
Wear and tear	(554)
Property income	2938

(b) Oliver and George jointly own a house, which is their main residence. They let out one of the rooms to Julie.

What is the maximum exempt amount to which Oliver and George are each entitled under rent a room relief?

	✓
£2,000	
£2,125	✓
£4,000	
£4,250	

Task 4

During 2015/16, Eva received the following income.

In each case, show the amount of income that she should enter on her tax return. If the income is exempt, enter 0.

(1) Employment income £20,000, tax deducted £2,700.

£  20 000

(2) Government stock ('gilt') interest £40.

£  40

(3) Interest on ISA account £90.

£  0

(4) Dividends received £1,152.

£ 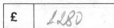 1280

Task 5

Denise works for Jules Ltd. She provides you with the following information:

(1) Annual salary £104,000 received on 25th day of each month

(2) Employer's contribution of 5% of salary on 31 December 2015 to company's occupational pension scheme. Denise contributes 4% of her salary into this scheme. 4160

(3) Bonus of £1,000 received 30 April 2015 based on company's accounting profit for the year ended 31 December 2014

(4) Bonus of £1,200 received 30 April 2016 based on company's accounting profit for the year ended 31 December 2015

(5) She has use of a company car for which the benefit in kind has been computed as £3,000. Denise pays for all the private petrol that she uses in this car.

(6) During 2015/16 Denise received £120 of bank interest and £50 of dividends from an ISA.

Complete the following table showing the figures that should be included in Denise's taxable income for 2015/16. You should use whole pounds only. If your answer is zero, please input a '0'. Do not use brackets or minus signs.

	£
Salary	104 000
Employer's pension contribution	0
Employee's pension contribution	(4 160)
Bonus received 30 April 2015	1 000
Bonus received 30 April 2016	0
Benefit in kind for car	3 000
Interest from bank	150
Dividends from ISA	0
Total income	103 990
Personal allowance	(8 605)
Taxable income	95 385

Task 6

(a) Elaine was born in 1968. During 2015/16 she earned £115,000 of employment income and received bank interest of £20,000 and dividends of £18,000.

Calculate her total income tax liability to the nearest pound for 2015/16, entering your answer and workings in the blank table given below. You have been given more space than you will need.

	NSI	SI	dividends
salary	115 000		
Bank interest		25 000	
dividends			20000
	115 000	25 000	20 000
PA > 121 200	0		
Basic 31 785 × 20 %	6357		
83 215 × 40 %	33 286		
25000 × 40%	10 000		
10 000 × 32,5%	3 250		
10 000 × 37,5%	3 750		
Total liability	56 643		

(b) Elaine is considering making a Gift Aid donation of £500 each year to a charity. However she does not understand the tax implications of doing this.

Explain to Elaine how she will get tax relief on such donations, and the tax implications if she had made a £500 Gift Aid donation during 2015/16.

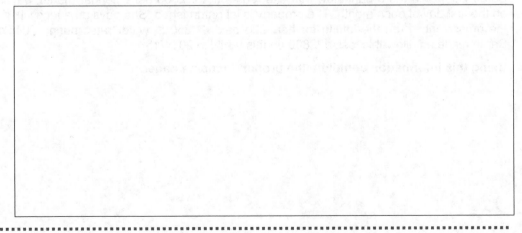

Task 7

Today's date is 15 January 2017.

Margaret filed her 2014/15 tax return online on 25 November 2016.

The assessment for 2014/15 showed a tax liability of £800, which has not yet been paid.

Discuss the penalties and interest that may be applied by HMRC on Margaret for both the late filing of the tax return and the late payment of tax. Explain how any outstanding tax for 2015/16 may be collected by HMRC, based on the information given above.

Task 8

Sarah Cartney owns a bungalow that she rents out for £500 per calendar month, payable on the first day of each month. The property is let unfurnished. She pays an agency 10% of the gross rent to run the letting for her. She paid £1,250 in water rates during 2015/16. Sarah made an allowable loss of £860 on this rental in 2014/15.

Using this information complete the property income page.

Property income

Do not include furnished holiday lettings, Real Estate Investment Trust or Property Authorised Investment Funds dividends/distributions here.

20 Total rents and other income from property £ 6 000 . 0 0	22 Premiums for the grant of a lease – form box E on the Worling Sheet – *read the notes* £ . 0 0
21 Tax taken off any income in box 20 £ . 0 0	23 Reverse premiums and inducements £ . 0 0

Property expenses

24 Rent, rates, insurance, ground rents etc. £ 1 2 5 0 . 0 0	27 Legal, management and other professional fees £ 6 0 0 . 0 0
25 Property repairs, maintenance and renewals £ . 0 0	28 Costs of services provided, including wages £ . 0 0
26 Loan interest and other financial costs £ . 0 0	29 Other allowable property expenses £ . 0 0

Calculating your taxable profit or loss

30 Private use adjustments – *read the notes* £ . 0 0	37 Rent a Room exempt amount £ . 0 0
31 Balancing charges – *read the notes* £ . 0 0	38 Adjusted profit for the year – from box O on the Working Sheet – *read the notes* £ 4 1 5 0 . 0 0
32 Annual Investment Allowance £ . 0 0	39 Loss brought forward used against this year's profits £ 8 6 0 . 0 0
33 Business Premises Renovation Allowance (Assisted Areas only) – *read the notes* £ . 0 0	40 Taxable profit for the year (box 38 minus box 39) £ 3 2 9 0 . 0 0
34 All other capital allowances £ . 0 0	41 Adjusted loss for the year – from box O on the Working Sheet – *read the notes* £ . 0 0
35 Landlord's Energy Saving Allowance £ . 0 0	42 Loss set off against 2015·16 total income – *this will be unusual – read the notes* £ . 0 0
36 10% wear and tear allowance – *for furnished residential accommodation only* £ . 0 0	43 Loss to carry forward to following year, including unused losses brought forward £ . 0 0

Task 9

(a) **For each of the following assets, tick whether they are chargeable or exempt assets for capital gains tax:**

Asset	Chargeable	Exempt
Car used solely for business purposes		✓
Holiday cottage	✓	
Vintage car worth £40,000		✓
Shares held in an individual savings account		✓

(b) Rodney purchased an antique chair for £1,450. On 10 October 2015 he sold the chair at auction for £6,300 (which was net of the auctioneer's 10% commission).

The chargeable gain on sale is: *7000*   Proceeds 7000

£ | *1667* |

(c) Andrew bought six acres of land for £405,000. He sold two acres of the land at auction for £360,000. His disposal costs were £6,000. The market value of the four remaining acres at the date of sale was £540,000.

(1) **The cost of the land sold is:**

£ | *162,000* |

(2) **The chargeable gain on sale is:**

£ | *192,000* |

....

cost $\dfrac{360\,000}{360\,000 + 540\,000} \times 405\,000 = 162\,000$

Proceeds -360 000
cost   6 000
          ‾‾‾‾‾‾‾‾
          354 000
          162 000
          ‾‾‾‾‾‾‾‾
          192 000

Task 10

In August 2010 Wayne acquired 4,000 shares in Main plc at a cost of £10,000. In September 2012, there was a one for one bonus issue when the shares were worth £8 each. Wayne sold 3,000 shares in July 2013 for £15,000, and purchased 3,000 back again October 2013 for 12,000.

Wayne sold half of his shareholding in June 2015 for £21,000.

Clearly showing the balance of shares and their value to carry forward, calculate the gain made on the sale of the shares in 2015/16. All workings must be shown in your calculations.

	Shares	Cost
August 2010	4000	10000
Sept 2012	4000	0
	8000	10000
July 2013 Disposal	(3000)	(3750)
3000/8000 × 10000	5000	6250
October 2013	3000	12000
	8000	18250
June 2015 disposal	(4000)	(9125)
4000/8000 × 18250		
c/f	4000	9125
Proceeds of sale	21 000	
Costs	(9125)	
Gain	11 875	

Task 11

(a) For each of the following statements, tick if they are True or False.

Any CGT annual exempt amount that is unused in one tax year can be carried forward to be used in the following tax year only.

True ☐

False ☑

Capital losses in a tax year must be offset against capital gains in that year, even if it means losing all, or some of the annual exempt amount.

True ☑

False ☐

(b) Charlotte bought a house on 1 February 2003 for £95,000 and sold it for £263,000 on 1 October 2015. During the period of ownership the following occurred:

01.02.03 to 31.10.05 3 2ws.	Charlotte lived in the property
01.11.05 to 31.03.14	Charlotte worked elsewhere in the UK
01.04.14 to 31.09.15	Charlotte lived in the property until she sold it

Input the correct answers in the boxes provided to complete the sentences. Where applicable round your answer to the nearest whole number.

263 000
(95 000)

The total period of ownership of the property is [152] months.

168 000)
(149 211)

The period of Charlotte's actual and deemed residence is [135] months.

The chargeable gain on the sale of the house is [18 789].

(c) Ella purchased an antique clock for £12,000. She sold it on 1 September 2015 for £62,100. Ella has no other chargeable assets. Her taxable income for 2015/16 was £29,385.

Ella's CGT payable for 2015/16 is:

£ [10680]

62 100
(12 000)

50 100
(11 100)

39 000

This is payable by (xx/xx/xxxx):

[31/01/17]

2400 x 18%
36 600 v 18% = 10 248   432   10680

BPP PRACTICE ASSESSMENT 1
PERSONAL TAX

ANSWERS

Task 1

(1) The cost of the car in the taxable benefit computation is:

£	16,700

(2) The percentage used in the taxable benefit computation is:

23	%

(140 – 95)/5 = 9% + 14% = 23%

(3) The taxable benefit in respect of the provision of fuel for private use is:

£	5,083

£22,100 × 23%

....

Task 2

(a)

(1) Mobile telephone

£	0

(2) Childcare vouchers

£	2,160

£(100 – 55) × 48

(3) Leisure club membership (cost to employer)

£	5,000

(4) Home (£5,900 + ((£227,000 – 75,000) × 3%))

£	10,460

(b)

Item	Wholly or partly taxable	Wholly exempt
Interest on loan of £8,000 (only loan provided)		✓ (£10,000 or less
Additional costs of home working of £5 per week (no evidence presented to employer)	✓ (evidence needed if more than £4 per week)	
Use of pool car		✓
One staff party costing £120 per head		✓ (up to £150)

Task 3

(a)

	£
Rent accrued £150 × 40	6,000
Expenses:	
Advertising	(190)
Water rates	(460)
Redecoration	(800)
Electricity	(690)
Cleaning	(368)
Central heating system (capital)	(0)
Wear and tear £(6,000 – 460) × 10%	(554)
Property income	2,938

(b)

	✓
£2,000	
£2,125	✓
£4,000	
£4,250	

The rent a room limit of £4,250 is halved if any other person also receives income from renting accommodation in the property.

....

Task 4

(1) Employment income £20,000, tax deducted £2,700.

£	20,000

(2) Government stock ('gilt') interest £40.(received gross).

£	40

(3) Interest on ISA account £90.

£	0

Exempt

(4) Dividends received £1,152.

£	1,280

£1,152 × 100/90

....

Task 5

	£
Salary	104,000
Employer's pension contribution (exempt)	0
Employee's pension contribution (£104,000 × 4%)	4,160
Bonus received 30 April 2015	1,000
Bonus received 30 April 2016	0
Benefit in kind for car	3,000
Interest from bank (£120 × 100/80)	150
Dividends from ISA (exempt)	0
Total income	103,990
Personal allowance £(10,600 – 1,995 (103,990 – 100,000)/2)	8,605
Taxable income	95,385

Task 6

(a)

	Non-savings £	Interest £	Dividends £
Employment Income	115,000		
Bank interest (£20,000 × 100/80)		25,000	
Dividends (£18,000 × 100/90)			20,000
Net income	115,000	25,000	20,000
Personal allowance (net income > £121,200)	(nil)		
Taxable income	115,000	25,000	20,000
£31,785 × 20%	6,357		
£83,215 (£115,000 – £31,785) × 40%	33,286		
£25,000 × 40%	10,000		
£10,000 × 32.5%	3,250		
£10,000 × 37.5%	3,750		
Income tax liability	56,643		

(b)

> If you make a Gift Aid donation of £500 each year to charity this amount will be grossed up at the basic rate of tax, giving a gross amount of £625.
>
> This gross figure of £625 will be used to extend the upper limit of the basic rate band to give an upper limit of £32,410 (£31,785 + £625) and will also extend the additional rate threshold to £150,625 (£150,000 + £625)
>
> This would mean that an extra £625 of your employment income would be taxed at the basic rate of tax of 20% instead of at the higher rate of tax of 40% and an extra £625 of your dividends would be taxed at the higher rate of tax of 32.5% instead of the additional rate of tax of 37.5%.

Task 7

> **Late return**
>
> Firstly, the return should have been filed by 31 January 2016. Margaret would receive an immediate fine of £100 for missing this date. As the return is more than three months late, HMRC may then charge a penalty of £10 per day (up to a maximum of 90 days) while the return is outstanding. As the return is also more than six months late, another penalty may arise which is the greater of £300 or 5% of the tax liability for the year.
>
> **Late payment**
>
> The £800 should have been paid by 31 January 2016. Interest would be incurred from the due date of payment to the actual date of payment. A penalty will also be imposed, being 10% of the tax outstanding as it is more than six months late.
>
> **2015/16**
>
> For 2015/16, as the income tax payable for 2014/15 is less than £1,000, payments on account will not be required. Instead, the tax for 2015/16 will all be due on 31 January 2017.

Task 8

Box 20 (£500 × 12)	6000.00
Box 24	1250.00
Box 27 (£6,000 × 10%)	600.00
Box 38	4150.00
Box 39	860.00
Box 40	3290.00

Task 9

(a)

Asset	Chargeable	Exempt
Car used solely for business purposes		✓
Holiday cottage	✓	
Vintage car worth £40,000		✓
Shares held in an individual savings account		✓

(b)

The chargeable gain on sale is:

£	1,667

	£
Disposal proceeds £6,300 × 100/90	7,000
Less disposal costs £7,000 × 10%	(700)
Net proceeds	6,300
Less cost	(1,450)
Gain	4,850
Cannot exceed 5/3 × £(7,000 − 6,000)	1,667

(c)

(1) The cost of the land sold is:

£	162,000

$$\frac{360,000}{360,000 + 540,000} \times £405,000$$

(2) The chargeable gain on sale is:

£	192,000

	£
Disposal proceeds	360,000
Less disposal costs	(6,000)
Net proceeds	354,000
Less cost	(162,000)
Chargeable gain	192,000

BPP
LEARNING MEDIA

Task 10

	£
Proceeds of sale	21,000
Less cost	(9,125)
Gain	11,875

	No. of shares	Cost £
August 2010 Acquisition	4,000	10,000
September 2012 Bonus 1 for 1	4,000	nil
	8,000	10,000
July 2013 Disposal (3,000/8,000 × £10,000)	(3,000)	(3,750)
	5,000	6,250
October 2013 Acquisition	3,000	12,000
	8,000	18,250
June 2015 Disposal (4,000/8,000 × £18,250)	(4,000)	(9,125)
c/f	4,000	9,125

Task 11

(a)

True ☐

False ☑

Any unused annual exempt amount is lost.

True ☑

False ☐

Only capital losses brought forward can be restricted to ensure the annual exempt amount isn't lost.

(b)

The total period of ownership of the property is [152] months.

The period of Charlotte's actual and deemed residence is [135] months.

01.02.03 – 31.10.05	33 months actual occupation
01.11.05 – 31.03.14	48 months – deemed occupation – working elsewhere in UK – preceded and followed by actual occupation
	36 months – deemed occupation – any reason – preceded and followed by actual occupation
	18 months non-occupation
01.04.14 – 31.09.15	18 months – actual occupation (last 18 months always deemed occupation anyway)

The chargeable gain on the sale of the house is [£18,789].

	£
Disposal proceeds	263,000
Less cost	(95,000)
	168,000
PPR £168,000 × 135/152	(149,211)
Chargeable gain	18,789

(c)

Ella's CGT payable for 2015/16 is:

£	10,680

This is payable by:

31/01/2017

	£
Disposal proceeds	62,100
Less cost	(12,000)
Gain	50,100
Less annual exempt amount	(11,100)
Taxable gain	39,000

CGT

	£
On £2,400 × 18% (unused basic rate band £31,785 – £29,385)	432
On £36,600 × 28%	10,248
	10,680

181

BPP PRACTICE ASSESSMENT 2
PERSONAL TAX

Time allowed: 2 hours

PRACTICE ASSESSMENT 2

TAXATION DATA

Taxation tables for personal tax – 2015/16

Note that 'TAXATION DATA 1' and 'TAXATION DATA 2' shown below will be available as pop-up windows throughout your live assessment.

TAXATION DATA 1

Pop-up 1

Tax rates and bands

	%	£
Basic rate	20	first 31,785
Higher rate	40	to 150,000
Additional rate	45	over 150,000

Savings income is taxed at 0%, 20%, 40% and 45%.

(0% applies to a maximum of £5,000 of savings income only where non-savings income is below this limit)

Dividends are taxed at 10%, 32.5% and 37.5%.

Personal allowances

	£
Personal allowance for individuals born after 5 April 1938	10,600
Age allowance for individuals born before 6 April 1938	10,660
Income limit for age allowance	27,700

TAXATION DATA 2
Pop-up 2

Car benefit percentage

Emission rating for petrol engines	%
0g/km to 50g/km	5
51g/km to 75g/km	9
76g/km to 94g/km	13
95g/km or more	14% + 1% for every extra 5g/km above 95g/km

Diesel engines – additional 3%

The figure for fuel is £22,100

Authorised mileage rates

First 10,000 miles	45p
Over 10,000 miles	25p

Van scale charge

	£
Charge	3,150
Private fuel provided	594
Low emission van charge	630

HMRC official rate
3%

Capital gains tax

Annual exempt amount	£11,100
Tax rate	18%
Higher rate	28%

Task 1

Steel Ltd provides Susan with two company cars during 2015/16 for private and business use. The first car cost £13,800 when new, has CO_2 emissions of 120g/km and has a diesel engine. The second car has a list price of £12,000, has CO_2 emissions of 90g/km and has a petrol engine. Susan used the first car for the first 7 months of 2015/16, and the second car for the remaining 5 months. Steel Ltd pays for all the running costs which amount to £950 for the first car and £735 for the second car. Steel also paid for private fuel for the second car, however Susan had to contribute £20 per month towards this.

(1) **The scale charge percentage for the first car is:**

22	%

(2) **The taxable benefit for the first car is:**

£	1771

(3) **The scale charge percentage for the second car is:**

13	%

(4) **The taxable benefit for the second car is:**

£	650

(5) **The fuel benefit for the second car is:**

£	1197

Task 2

(a) **Which ONE of the following is not a wholly exempt employment benefit?**

	✓
Long service award of £900 to employee with 30 years of service	
Workplace parking	
Workplace childcare facilities	
Moving expenses of £10,000	√

(b) **For each of the following benefits provided to Emily by her employer Bloom Ltd, calculate the amount of the taxable benefit for 2015/16. If a benefit is exempt, enter 0.**

(1) Bloom Ltd gave Emily a loan on 1 August 2015 of £6,000 to pay for home improvements. Emily pays the company 1% interest on the loan, but has not repaid any of the loan itself.

The taxable benefit for 2015/16 is:

£ | 0

(2) On 1 May 2015 Bloom Ltd provided her with a mobile telephone costing £150 for private and business use.

The taxable benefit for 2015/16 is:

£ | 0

(c) Bella's employer provided her with a house on 1 April 2015, when it was valued at £125,000. The employer had bought the house for £80,000 on 1 April 2006. The annual value of the house is £1,500. Bella pays £75 a month to the employer for the use of the house. She is also provided with new furniture valued at £15,000 on 1 April 2015.

(1) The **basic accommodation benefit for 2015/16 is:**

£ | 600

(2) **The cost of providing the accommodation for calculating the additional benefit is:**

£ | 125000

(3) **The additional accommodation benefit for 2015/16 is:**

£ | 1500

(4) **The benefit for provision of furniture for 2015/16 is:**

£ | 3000

Task 3

(a) Demi bought two properties on 1 July 2015.

Property 1 was let unfurnished from 1 September 2015 at an annual rent of £12,000 payable monthly in arrears. The rent due on 31 March 2016 was not received until 14 April 2016.

The following were expenses paid by Demi on the property:

		£
1 July 2015	Insurance for the year ended 30 June 2016	700
8 Sept 2015	Accountancy fees	100
25 January 2016	Re-painting the exterior of the property	400

Property 2 was let furnished from 1 August 2015 at an annual rent of £9,000 payable annually in advance.

The following were expenses paid by Demi on the property:

		£
1 July 2015	Insurance for the year ended 30 June 2016	800
31 March 2016	Redecoration	900

Using the proforma layout provided, calculate Demi's property income for the tax year 2015/16 by filling in the unshaded boxes. Add zeros if necessary. Both brackets and minus signs can be used to show negative numbers.

	Property 1 £	Property 2 £
Rental income		
Property 1	7000	
Property 2		6000
Less expenses		
Insurance	(525)	(600)
Accountancy	(100)	0
Repainting	(400)	0
Redecoration	0	(900)
Wear and tear allowance	0	(600)
Net income	5975	3900
Total property income 2015/16	9875	

(b) **Which ONE of the following is not a condition for a property to be qualifying holiday accommodation?**

The property is furnished	
The property must be actually let for at least 105 days during the same tax year	
The property must be available for letting to the public as holiday accommodation for at least 210 days in the tax year	
The property must be situated in the UK	√

Task 4

Sarah receives a dividend of £7,200 on 10 December 2015.

(1) **The gross amount of the dividend is:**

£   8000

(2) **The tax credit attaching to the dividend is:**

£   800

(3) **Sarah will receive a repayment if the tax credit exceeds her income tax liability**

True ☐

False ☑

Paul receives interest of £5,000 from an ISA and £3,500 of building society interest during 2015/16.

(4) **His gross amount of savings income for 2015/16 is:**

£   4375

(5) **The tax deducted at source is:**

£   875

(6) **Paul will receive a repayment of the tax deducted at source if it exceeds his income tax liability**

True ☑

False ☐

Task 5

(a) Gavin is employed by XYZ plc. For each of the following payments, state the amount of employment income taxable in 2015/16. If an amount is not taxable in 2015/16 enter 0.

(1) Annual salary received in monthly payments on the last working day of each month. Until the end of December 2015, his annual salary was £36,000. He had a 2% annual pay increase with effect from 1 January 2016.

The salary to be included in employment income for 2015/16 is:

£ _36 180_

(2) Bonus of £2,000 received 31 March 2016 based on company's accounting profit for the year ended 31 December 2015.

The bonus to be included in employment income for 2015/16 is:

£ _2000_

(3) Commission of £500 received 30 April 2016 on sales made in the month of March 2016.

The commission to be included in employment income for 2015/16 is:

£ _0_

(4) Employer's contribution of £5,000 on 10 March 2016 towards Gavin's occupational pension scheme.

The benefit to be included in employment income for 2015/16 is:

£ _0_

(b) Your client Jackie, who was born in March 1969, received the following income in 2015/16:

	£
Trading income	20,000
Property income	5,000
Building society interest	_145_ 116
Interest from government stocks	180
Interest from an ISA	204
Dividends	_210_ 189

(1) **Jackie's total non-savings income for 2015/16 is:**

£  _25 000_

(2) **Jackie's total savings income for 2015/16 is:**

£  _325_

(3) **Jackie's total dividend income for 2015/16 is:**

£ | 210

....

Task 6

(a) Donald has the following amounts of taxable income (AFTER deduction of his personal allowance) for 2015/16:

Non-savings income £152,395 (PAYE deducted £52,000)
Savings income £145 (Tax deducted at source £29)
Dividend income £210 (Tax credit £21)

Donald's tax liability on each source of income for 2015/16 is as follows:

(1) Non-savings income:

£ | 54721

(2) Savings income:

£ | 65

(3) Dividend income:

£ | 79

(4) Donald's tax payable for 2015/16 is:

£ | 2815

(b) You have received the following email from Serena Miles:

From:	SMiles@webmail.net
To:	AATStudent@boxmail.net
Sent:	30 November 2016
Subject:	Pensions

I currently don't have a pension and I am worried about this. I have two options. My employer, ABC plc, has said that I can join their occupational pension scheme. This would involve me paying 5% of my basic salary, and they would pay another 7%. However, I don't know how long I am going to continue to work for them.

Alternatively, I am thinking of taking out a private pension, possibly paying about 6% of my earnings into it.

However, I have no idea about the tax implications of these schemes. Would I get tax relief, and if so, how?

I hope you can help.

Serena

WITHOUT discussing the merits of each scheme, advise Serena on the tax implications of an occupational pension scheme and a private pension scheme.

From:	AATStudent@boxmail.net
To:	SMiles@webmail.net
Sent:	1 December 2016
Subject:	Pensions

Task 7

Julie has income tax payable for 2015/16 of £4,215. She was not required to make any payments on account.

(1) **The date by which the tax payable should be paid is: (insert date as xx/xx/xxxx)**

 31 /01 / 2017

(2) **Each payment on account for 2016/17 is:**

£   2107   .   50

(3) **The dates by which the payments on account for 2016/17 should be paid are: (insert dates as xx/xx/xxxx)**

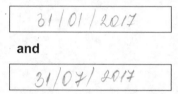 31 / 01 / 2017

and

31 /07 / 2017

(4) Julie is a higher rate taxpayer. She has omitted to include £1,500 of building society income (gross) in her return for 2015/16.

Assuming that the error is a deliberate error without concealment but Julie makes disclosure of the error without prompting, the minimum penalty for error that will be imposed is:

£   60

Task 8

You act for Ricky Fernandez, who is employed by PQR plc. He has provided you with the following information about his employment in 2015/16:

PQR plc

	£
Salary paid	30,000
Tax taken off	4,700
Company car benefit	4,500
Fuel benefit	2,400
Professional subscription paid by Ricky	300

Using this information complete the employment income page.

Employment

Tax year 6 April 2015 to 5 April 2016

Your name
Licky Fernandez

Your unique taxpayer reference (UTR)

Complete an *Employment* page for each employment or directorship

1 Pay from this employment - the total from your P45 or P60 - *before tax was taken off*
£ 30000.00

2 UK tax taken off pay in box 1
£ 4700.00

3 Tips and other payments not on your P60 - *read page EN 3 of the notes*

4 PAYE tax reference of your employer (on your P45/P60)

5 Your employer's name
PQR plc

6 If you were a company director, put 'X' in the box

7 And, if the company was a close company, put 'X' in the box

8 If you are a part-time teacher in England or Wales and are on the Repayment of Teachers' Loans Scheme for this employment, put 'X' in the box

Benefits from your employment - use your form P11D (or equivalent information)

9 Company cars and vans - *the total 'cash equivalent' amount*
£ 4500.00

10 Fuel for company cars and vans - *the total 'cash equivalent' amount*
£ 2400.00

11 Private medical and dental insurance - *the total 'cash equivalent' amount*

12 Vouchers, credit cards and excess mileage allowance

13 Goods and other assets provided by your employer - *the total value or amount*

14 Accommodation provided by your employer - *the total value or amount*

15 Other benefits (including interest-free and low interest loans) - *the total 'cash equivalent' amount*

16 Expenses payments received and balancing charges

Employment expenses

17 Business travel and subsistence expenses

18 Fixed deductions for expenses

19 Professional fees and subscriptions
£ 300.00

20 Other expenses and capital allowances

Shares schemes, employment lump sums, compensation, deductions and Seafarers' Earnings Deduction are on the *Additional information* pages enclosed in the tax return pack

SA102 2014 | Tax return: Employment: Page E 1 | HMRC 12/13

Task 9

(a) Classify whether a disposal of each of the following assets will be chargeable to or exempt from capital gains tax:

Asset	Chargeable	Exempt
Shares in XYZ plc held in an ISA	☐	☑
Ruby necklace valued at £100,000	☑	☐
Vintage Rolls Royce Car	☐	☑
Factory used in a trade	☑	☐

(b) Trevor bought a 5 acre plot of land for £50,000. He sold 3 acres of the land at auction for £105,000 in August 2015. He had spent £2,500 installing drainage on the 3 acres which he sold. His disposal costs were £1,500. The market value of the remaining 2 acres at the date of sale was £45,000.

The gain on sale of the 3 acres is:

	✓
£66,000	√
£66,750	
£71,000	
£66,152	

(c)

(1) Matt bought a picture for £7,000 and had costs of acquisition of £300. He sold it in August 2015 for £4,500 and had costs of disposal of £200.

The allowable loss on sale is: (either show the loss by using brackets or a minus sign)

£	1500

(2) Keith bought a greyhound for £5,000. It won a number of races and he sold it for £7,000 in December 2015, incurring costs of disposal of £250.

The chargeable gain on sale is:

	✓
Nil	√
£1,667	
£1,250	
£1,750	

Task 10

Lee had the following transactions in shares in Snowy Ltd:

Acquisitions	No of shares	Cost £
December 2006	10,000	10,800
August 2007	Bonus, 1 for 1	Nil
June 2011	10,000	8,700
December 2011	Rights Issue, 1 for 10	40p each

Disposal		Proceeds £
September 2015	15,000	18,650

Using the proforma layout provided, calculate the chargeable gain made on the disposal of the shares in Snowy Ltd, and show the balance of shares to be carried forward for future disposal. Fill in all unshaded boxes, enter 0 if appropriate. Both brackets and minus signs can be used to show negative numbers.

Gain

	£
Proceeds of sale	18 650
Less cost	(9409)
Chargeable gain	9241

Share pool

	No of shares	Cost £
December 2006 Acquisition	10 000	10 800
August 2007 Bonus issue	10 000	0
	20 000	10 800
June 2011 Acquisition	10 000	8 700
	30 000	19 500
December 2011 Rights issue	3 000	1 200
	33 000	20 700
September 2015 Disposal	(15 000)	(9409)
c/f	18 000	11 291

Task 11

Irma had the following chargeable gains in 2015/16:

Gain on sale of shares August 2015	£9,341
Gain on sale of furniture February 2016	£4,167
She had allowable losses brought forward of	£1,000

Irma is an additional rate taxpayer.

(1) **Irma's taxable gains for 2015/16 are:**

£ _1408_

(2) **Irma's CGT payable for 2015/16 is:**

£ _394_

(3) **Irma's CGT is due for payment by: (enter date as xx/xx/xxxx)**

_31 /01/ 2017_

BPP PRACTICE ASSESSMENT 2
PERSONAL TAX

ANSWERS

Task 1

(1) The scale charge percentage for the first car is:

22	%

120g/km – 95g/km = 25/5 = 5% + 14% + 3%

(2) The taxable benefit for the first car is:

£	1,771

£13,800 × 22% × 7/12

(3) The scale charge percentage for the second car is:

13	%

(Between 76g/km and 94g/km)

(4) The taxable benefit for the second car is:

£	650

£12,000 × 13% × 5/12

(5) The fuel benefit for the second car is:

£	1,197

£22,100 × 13% × 5/12

Task 2

(a)

	✓
Long service award of £900 to employee with 30 years of service	
Workplace parking	
Workplace childcare facilities	
Moving expenses of £10,000	✓

Moving expenses of £10,000 are only exempt up to £8,000, the excess is taxable.

The long service award is wholly exempt as it is within the limit of £50 for each year of service and the period of service is in excess of 20 years.

(b)

(1) The taxable benefit for 2015/16 is:

£	0

No taxable benefit arises if the combined outstanding balance on all loans to the employee did not exceed £10,000 at any time in the tax year.

(2) The taxable benefit for 2015/16 is:

£	0

Exempt

(c)

(1) The basic accommodation benefit for 2015/16 is:

£	600

	£
Annual value	1,500
Less payment by employee £75 × 12 =	(900)
Basic accommodation benefit	600

(2) The cost of providing the accommodation for calculating the additional benefit is:

£	125,000

Market value at provision (acquired more than 6 years before provision)

(3) The additional accommodation benefit for 2015/16 is:

£	1,500

Excess of £125,000 over £75,000 = £50,000 × 3%

(4) The benefit for provision of furniture for 2015/16 is:

£	3,000

£15,000 × 20%

Task 3

(a)

	Property 1	Property 2
	£	£
Rental income		
Property 1 £12,000 × 7/12	7,000	
Property 2 £9,000 × 8/12		6,000
Less expenses		
Insurance £700 / £800 × 9/12	(525)	(600)
Accountancy	(100)	0
Repainting	(400)	0
Redecoration	0	(900)
Wear and tear allowance £6,000 × 10%	0	(600)
Net income	5,975	3,900
Total property income 2015/16	9,875	

(b)

	✓
The property is furnished	
The property must be actually let for at least 105 days during the same tax year	
The property must be available for letting to the public as holiday accommodation for at least 210 days in the tax year	
The property must be situated in the UK	✓

The property must be situated in the European Economic Area (which includes the UK).

....

Task 4

(1) The gross amount of the dividend is:

£	8,000

£7,200 × 100/90

(2) The tax credit attaching to the dividend is:

£	800

£8,000 × 10%

(3) True ☐

False ☑

The tax credit can only be used to reduce Sarah's tax liability to nil, it cannot be repaid.

(4) His gross amount of savings income for 2015/16 is:

£	4,375

£3,500 × 100/80 = £4,375. ISA interest is exempt income

(5) The tax deducted at source is:

£	875

£4,375 × 20%

(6) Paul will receive a repayment of the tax deducted at source if it exceeds his income tax liability

True ☑

False ☐

Task 5

(a)

(1) The salary to be included in employment income for 2015/16 is:

£ | 36,180

	£
Salary April to December 2015 9/12 × £36,000	27,000
Salary January to March 2016 3/12 × £(36,000 × 102%)	9,180

(2) The bonus to be included in employment income for 2015/16 is:

£ | 2,000

Bonus received 31 March 2016

(3) The commission to be included in employment income for 2015/16 is:

£ | 0

Commission received 30 April 2016 (taxable in 2016/17)

(4) The benefit to be included in employment income for 2015/16 is:

£ | 0

Exempt benefit

(b)

(1) Jackie's total non-savings income for 2015/16 is:

£ | 25,000

£20,000 + £5,000

(2) Jackie's total savings income for 2015/16 is:

£ | 325

(£116 × 100/80) + £180 = £325

(3) Jackie's total dividend income for 2015/16 is:

£ | 210

£189 × 100/90

Task 6

(a)

(1) Non-savings income:

£	54,721

	£
£31,785 × 20%	6,357
£118,215 × 40%	47,286
£2,395 × 45%	1,078
£152,395	54,721

(2) Savings income:

£	65

£145 × 45%

(3) Dividend income:

£	79

£210 × 37.5%

(4) Donald's tax payable for 2015/16 is:

£	2,815

	£
Income tax liability £(54,721 + 65 + 79)	54,865
Less dividend tax credit	(21)
Interest: tax deducted at source	(29)
PAYE	(52,000)
Income tax payable	2,815

(b)

From:	AATStudent@boxmail.net
To:	SMiles@webmail.net
Sent:	1 December 2016
Subject:	Pensions

Occupational pension schemes operate by the employer deducting your pension contribution from your salary before the PAYE is calculated. In your case this would be 5%. This means that full tax relief is automatically obtained at source at your applicable rate of tax. The employer is responsible for paying over the pension payments to the pension provider.

The 7% that your employer pays to the pension scheme on your behalf has no tax implications for you, ie this will not be classed as a taxable benefit.

Private pension schemes work quite differently. You pay the pension provider direct, usually monthly. The amount you pay is net of basic rate tax.

So if for example, you decide you would like to put £100 a month into your pension, you only actually have to pay in £80, HM Revenue & Customs will pay the other £20. This automatically provides you with 20% tax relief.

If however, you are a higher or additional rate taxpayer, you will be entitled to further tax relief. In order to get tax relief at the higher rate of 40% or the additional rate of 45%, the basic rate band (and also the additional rate threshold) is extended by the gross pension contributions so that the 40% and 45% tax rates will apply after the pension has been adjusted for.

Task 7

(1) The date by which the tax payable should be paid is:

31/01/2017

(2) Each payment on account for 2016/17 is:

£	2,107	.	50

£4,215 ÷ 2

(3) The dates by which the payments on account for 2016/17 should be paid are:

31/01/2017

and

31/07/2017

(4) Potential lost revenue £1,500 × 20% = £300 (20% tax already suffered at source)

Minimum penalty for deliberate, not concealed error with unprompted disclosure is:

£	60

20% × £300

Task 8

Name	Ricky Fernandez
Box 1	30000.00
Box 2	4700.00
Box 5	PQR plc
Box 9	4500.00
Box 10	2400.00
Box 19	300.00

Task 9

(a)

Asset	Chargeable	Exempt
Shares in XYZ plc held in an ISA		✓
Ruby necklace valued at £100,000	✓	
Vintage Rolls Royce Car		✓
Factory used in a trade	✓	

(b)

	✓
£66,000	✓
£66,750	
£71,000	
£66,152	

	£
Proceeds of sale	105,000
Less costs of disposal	(1,500)
Net proceeds	103,500
Less cost	
(105,000/105,000 + 45,000) × £50,000	(35,000)
enhancement expenditure	(2,500)
Chargeable gain	66,000

(c)

(1) The allowable loss on sale is:

£	(1,500)

	£
Deemed disposal proceeds	6,000
Less costs of disposal	(200)
Net deemed disposal proceeds	5,800
Less cost £(7,000 + 300)	(7,300)
Allowable loss	(1,500)

(2)

	✓
Nil	✓
£1,667	
£1,250	
£1,750	

The greyhound is a wasting chattel and so is an exempt asset. Therefore there is no chargeable gain on the disposal.

Task 10

Gain

	£
Proceeds of sale	18,650
Less cost	(9,409)
Chargeable gain	9,241

Share pool

	No of shares	Cost £
December 2006 Acquisition	10,000	10,800
August 2007 Bonus 1 for 1	10,000	0
	20,000	10,800
June 2011 Acquisition	10,000	8,700
	30,000	19,500
December 2011 Rights 1 for 10 × £0.40	3,000	1,200
	33,000	20,700
September 2015 Disposal (15,000/33,000 × £20,700)	(15,000)	(9,409)
c/f	18,000	11,291

Task 11

(1) Irma's taxable gains for 2015/16 are:

£	1,408

	£
Gain on shares	9,341
Gain on furniture	4,167
	13,508
Less loss brought forward	(1,000)
Net chargeable gains	12,508
Less annual exempt amount	(11,100)
Taxable gains	1,408

(2) Irma's CGT payable for 2015/16 is:

£	394

£1,408 × 28%

(3) Irma's CGT is due for payment by:

31/01/2017

BPP PRACTICE ASSESSMENT 3
PERSONAL TAX

Time allowed: 2 hours

TAXATION DATA

Taxation tables for personal tax – 2015/16

Note that 'TAXATION DATA 1' and 'TAXATION DATA 2' shown below will be available as pop-up windows throughout your live assessment.

TAXATION DATA 1

Pop-up 1

Tax rates and bands

	%	£
Basic rate	20	first 31,785
Higher rate	40	to 150,000
Additional rate	45	over 150,000

Savings income is taxed at 0%, 20%, 40% and 45%.

(0% applies to a maximum of £5,000 of savings income only where non-savings income is below this limit)

Dividends are taxed at 10%, 32.5% and 37.5%.

Personal allowances

	£
Personal allowance for individuals born after 5 April 1938	10,600
Age allowance for individuals born before 6 April 1938	10,660
Income limit for age allowance	27,700

TAXATION DATA 2

Pop-up 2

Car benefit percentage

Emission rating for petrol engines	%
0g/km to 50g/km	5
51g/km to 75g/km	9
76g/km to 94g/km	13
95g/km or more	14% + 1% for every extra 5g/km above 95g/km

Diesel engines – additional 3%

The figure for fuel is £22,100

Authorised mileage rates

First 10,000 miles	45p
Over 10,000 miles	25p

Van scale charge

	£
Charge	3,150
Private fuel provided	594
Low emission van charge	630

HMRC official rate

3%

Capital gains tax

Annual exempt amount	£11,100
Tax rate	18%
Higher rate	28%

Task 1

Khalid works for KML plc, and is provided with a company car for business and private use from 6 June 2015. *10m*

The car has a diesel engine with CO_2 emissions of 162g/km. It has a list price of £27,000, although the company actually paid £23,500 for the car. Khalid agreed to make a capital contribution of £6,000 towards the cost of the car. The company pays for all running costs, including all fuel. Khalid pays £50 a month towards the cost of private fuel – the actual cost of private fuel is about £90 a month. *max coul 5000*

(1) **The cost of the car in the taxable benefit computation is:**

£21,000	
£22,000	√
£17,500	
£18,500	

(2) **The percentage used in the taxable benefit computation is:**

30	%

(3) **The taxable benefit in respect of the provision of fuel for private use is:**

£	5525

....

Task 2

(a) Lou is employed by Jane Quentin and receives the following benefits as the result of her employment.

In each case enter the taxable benefit arising. Enter 0 if the benefit is not taxable.

(1) An interest free loan of £10,500 made on 1 July 2015, no repayments made during 2015/16

£	236

(2) Cash voucher for £100 provided in December 2015. Jane acquired the voucher for £90

£	100

(3) Van for business and private use from 1 October 2015 onwards

| £ | 1575 | *6m.*
|---|---|

(4) Fuel for van for private use from 1 January 2016 onwards

£	149

(b) For each of the following benefits, tick whether they would be partly exempt or wholly exempt if received by an employee who is a basic rate taxpayer in 2015/16:

Benefit	Partly exempt	Wholly exempt
Staff party costing £125 per head		✓
Childcare vouchers of £55 per week		✓
Removal expenses of £10,000	✓	
Work related training costing £1,500		✓

(c) Madge is employed by V plc. She uses her own car for business purposes and is reimbursed 45p per mile by her employer. Madge travelled 15,000 miles on business in 2015/16.

What are the employment income consequences of the reimbursement for business mileage?

	✓
£6,750 taxable benefit	
£1,000 taxable benefit	✓
No taxable benefit or allowable deduction	
£1,000 allowable deduction	

6750
(4500)
/1250/
1000 tax

Task 3

(a) Michaela rents out a house from 1 July 2015. *9m*

She charges a rent of £600 per month payable in arrears on the last day of each month. The tenants don't pay the rent due on 31 March 2016 until 10 April 2016.

Michaela also pays an insurance premium of £400 on 6 July 2015, covering the period
6 July 2015 to 5 July 2016.

(1) **The rental income taxable for 2015/16 is:**

£ | 5400

(2) **The insurance premium allowable as an expense for 2015/16 is:**

£ | 300

(b) Wilma owns two flats that she rents out. Flat A is unfurnished. Flat B is furnished. The income and expenses for these properties are:

	Flat A *unf* £	Flat B *furn* £
Monthly income:		
Rent	500	650
Annual expenses:		
Council tax	1,000	800
Water rates	300	300
Insurance	350	250

Flat A was fully occupied during 2015/16. However, the tenants in Flat B moved out in November 2016, having paid the rent to the end of that month. Wilma was unable to re-let the flat until June 2016.

Wilma claims the wear and tear allowance as appropriate.

Wilma had a loss of £1,200 on her income from property in 2014/15.

Using the proforma layout below, calculate Wilma's property income for 2015/16. Fill in all unshaded boxes, enter 0 if appropriate. Both brackets and minus signs can be used to show negative numbers.

	Flat A £	Flat B £
Income	6000	5200
Expenses:		
Council tax	(1000)	(800)
Water rates	(300)	(300)
Insurance	(350)	(250)
Wear and tear	0	(410)
Net income from property	4350	3440
Total property income	7790	
Less loss b/f	(1200)	
Taxable property income	6590	

(c) Olga owns two furnished cottages which she lets out as follows:

	Blue Cottage	Green Cottage
Days available for letting in 2015/16	195	255
Days actually let in 2015/16	106	100

Tick to show which of the properties could be qualifying holiday accommodation.

	✓
Blue Cottage only	
Green Cottage only	
Both Blue Cottage and Green Cottage	
Neither Blue Cottage nor Green Cottage	√

Task 4

(a) Using the proforma layout provided, show whether the following amounts of interest are received net of basic rate tax or gross by an individual taxpayer:

Loan stock from company
Building society fixed rate bond
Bank deposit account
Government loan stock ('gilts')

Received net	Received gross
остальное	Gilts

(b) Tick the relevant box to show which of the following types of income are chargeable to income tax and which are exempt from income tax:

Source of income	Chargeable	Exempt
Individual Savings Account interest		✓
Government stock interest	✓	
Dividends received from an Individual Savings Account		✓
Bank deposit account interest	✓	

Task 5

(a) The following amounts were received in relation to employment:

(a) Monthly salary of £1,500 paid on the last working day of each month

(b) Tips of £300 paid by customers directly to an employee

(c) Employer's contribution of 6% of salary to company's occupational pension scheme

(d) Reimbursement of business expenses of £500 – a dispensation is in force for such payments

For each item, tick either taxable or not taxable:

Item	Taxable	Not taxable
Salary	✓	☐
Tips	✓	☐
Employer's pension contribution	☐	✓
Reimbursement of business expenses	☐	✓

(b) Eric Wright was born in September 1959 and is employed as an architect. His employment income for 2015/16 was £96,870 and PAYE of £28,500 was deducted at source.

Eric has a bank account with the Halifax Bank. His account was credited with interest of £1,600 on 31 March 2016.

Eric received a dividend of £6,750 on 1 July 2015.

Eric made a Gift Aid donation of £400 to Oxfam on 1 December 2015. *500*

Using the proforma layout provided, prepare a schedule of Eric's taxable income for 2015/16, clearly showing the distinction between non-savings, savings and dividend income. Both brackets and minus signs can be used to show negative numbers.

	Non-Savings income £	Savings income £	Dividend income £	Total £
Salary	96870			96870
Bank interest		2000		2000
Dividend			7500	7500
Net income	96870	2000	7500	106370
Less PA	(7665)			(7665)
Taxable income	89205	2000	7500	98705

Task 6

(a) Guy was born on 14 March 1978 and has the following income for 2015/16:

	£	
Employment income (PAYE £250)	11,250	
Interest received from building societies	37,000	*46250*
Dividends received	12,500	*13889*

Calculate Guy's income tax payable for 2015/16 entering your answer and workings into the blank table below. Brackets or a minus sign are both acceptable when entering negative numbers.

	Non-savings	Savings	Dividends
Salary	11250		
Interest		46250	
Dividends			13 889
Less PA	(10 600)		
Taxable income	650	46250	13 889
Income tax			
650 × 20%	130		
4350 × 0%	0		
26785 × 20%	5357		
15115 × 40%	6046		
13 889 × 32.5%	4514		
Tax liability	16047	(250 + 9250 + 1389)²	
Tax payable	5158		

(b) Guy is considering asking his employer to set up a small charitable donation of about £50 a month and deduct it out of his salary, but is unsure if he will get any tax relief for this.

Explain to Guy how he will get tax relief on such donations.

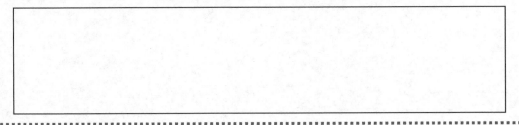

Task 7

(a) Owen is employed by X Ltd throughout 2015/16. He earns £35,000 a year. He also receives interest income from Santander Bank.

Until what date does Owen have to retain his records for tax for 2015/16?

	✓
All records until 31 January 2018	↲
Employment record until 31 January 2018, interest record until 31 January 2022	
Employment record until 31 January 2022, interest record until 31 January 2018	
All records until 31 January 2022	

(b) You receive the following email from a client, who is a higher rate taxpayer.

From:	Raman99@sherbet.net
To:	AATStudent@boxmail.net
Sent:	20 June 2016
Subject:	More information

Hello, I am so sorry, I know that you have already sent in my tax form for 2015/16. Unfortunately, I have forgotten to tell you that I made payments of £3,000 into my personal pension scheme.

Will I have to a pay a penalty for filing an incorrect return? What is the effect on my tax liability for 2015/16?

I hope you can help me, as I feel rather worried.

Thanks.

Raman

Reply to Raman's email.

From:	AATStudent@boxmail.net
To:	Raman99@sherbet.net
Sent:	22 June 2016
Subject:	More information

Task 8

Your client, Kara Allen, has given you the following information about her capital gains position for 2015/16:

Asset sold	Proceeds	Cost
Listed shares in OPQ plc	£10,000	£8,000
Unlisted shares in K Ltd	£15,500	£16,000
Painting	£17,000	£4,000

She also had losses brought forward from 2014/15 of £7,700.

Using this information, complete the capital gains summary on the next page.

HM Revenue & Customs

Capital gains summary
Tax year 6 April 2015 to 5 April 2016

1	Your name	2	Your Unique Taxpayer Reference (UTR)
	Kara Allen		

Summary of your enclosed computations

Please read the *Capital gains summary notes* before filling in this section. **You must enclose your computations, including details of each gain or loss, as well as filling in the boxes.**

ℹ️ To get notes and helpsheets that will help you fill in this form, go to hmrc.gov.uk/selfassessmentforms

3 Total gains *(Boxes 21 + 27 + 33 + 34)*
£ *15000* · 0 0

4 Gains qualifying for Entrepreneurs' Relief (but excluding gains deferred from before 23 June 2010) - *read the notes*
£ · 0 0

5 Gains invested under Seed Enterprise Investment Scheme and qualifying for exemption - *read the notes*
£ · 0 0

6 Total losses of the year - *enter '0' if there are none*
£ *500* · 0 0

7 Losses brought forward and used in the year
£ *3400* · 0 0

8 Adjustment to Capital Gains Tax - *read the notes*
£ — · 0 0

9 Additional liability for non-resident or dual resident trusts
£ · 0 0

10 Losses available to be carried forward to later years
£ *4300* · 0 0 ?

11 Losses used against an earlier year's gain (special circumstances apply - *read the notes*)
£ · 0 0

12 Losses used against income – amount claimed against 2015–16 income - *read the notes*
£ · 0 0

13 Amount in box 12 relating to shares to which Enterprise Investment Scheme/Seed Enterprise Investment Scheme relief is attributable
£ · 0 0

14 Losses used against income – amount claimed against 2014–15 income - *read the notes*
£ · 0 0

15 Amount in box 14 relating to shares to which Enterprise Investment Scheme/Seed Enterprise Investment Scheme relief is attributable
£ · 0 0

16 Income losses of 2015–16 set against gains
£ · 0 0

17 Deferred gains from before 23 June 2010 qualifying for Entrepreneurs' Relief
£ · 0 0

4800

3900

BPP LEARNING MEDIA

Listed shares and securities

18 Number of disposals - *read the notes*

`1`

19 Disposal proceeds

£ `1 0 0 0 0 . 0 0`

20 Allowable costs (including purchase price)

£ `8 0 0 0 . 0 0`

21 Gains in the year, before losses

£ `2 0 0 0 . 0 0`

22 If you are making any claim or election, put 'X' in the box

23 If your computations include any estimates or valuations, put 'X' in the box

Unlisted shares and securities

24 Number of disposals - *read the notes*

`1`

25 Disposal proceeds

£ `1 5 5 0 0 . 0 0`

26 Allowable costs (including purchase price)

£ `1 6 0 0 0 . 0 0`

27 Gains in the year, before losses

£ `0 . 0 0`

28 If you are making any claim or election, put 'X' in the box

29 If your computations include any estimates or valuations, put 'X' in the box

Property and other assets and gains

30 Number of disposals

`1`

31 Disposal proceeds

£ `1 7 0 0 0 . 0 0`

32 Allowable costs (including purchase price)

£ `4 0 0 0 . 0 0`

33 Gains in the year, before losses

£ `1 3 0 0 0 . 0 0`

34 Attributed gains where personal losses cannot be set off

£ `. 0 0`

35 If you are making any claim or election, put 'X' in the box

36 If your computations include any estimates or valuations, put 'X' in the box

Any other information

37 Please give any other information in this space

Task 9

(a) For each statement, tick the appropriate box in respect of the capital gains calculation:

Disposal	Market value used	Actual proceeds used	No gain/no loss disposal
Olivia sells shares for £5,000 to her wife Lucy when they are worth £4,000	☐	☐	☑
William sells land to his brother for £10,000 when it is worth £50,000	☑	☐	☐
Zeta gives an asset worth £4,000 to her friend Tanya	☑	☐	☐
Olwyn sells listed shares for proceeds of £12,000	☐	☑	☐

(b) Melly bought a holiday cottage for £32,000, incurring legal costs of £600 on the purchase. She spent £6,000 on adding a conservatory to the cottage. This was destroyed during a storm in 2013 and not replaced. Melly sold the cottage in March 2016 for £45,000. She paid estate agent's fees of £900 and legal costs of £350.

The chargeable gain on sale is:

£ _11 150_

(c)

(1) Suki purchased a vase for £9,500. In December 2015 she sold the vase at auction for £2,500. This amount is before deducting the auctioneer's 10% commission. _250 commis._

The allowable loss on sale is:

	✓
£3,750	✓
£3,500	
£7,000	
£7,250	

_600 0_
_(250)_
_5 750_
_(9 500)_

(2) **A chattel with a useful life of 60 years or less is a wasting chattel.**

True ☐

False ☑

Task 10

Vernon sold 4,000 shares in R Ltd for £36,200 on 23 February 2016. He had acquired his holdings in R Ltd as follows:

Date	Transaction	No of shares	£
14 April 2001	Purchase	6,000	18,400
29 May 2006	Rights issue	1 for 20	£4 each
10 March 2016	Purchase	500	3,400

Using the proforma layout provided, compute the total gain on sale. Both brackets and minus signs can be used to show negative numbers.

Share pool

	No of shares	Cost £
14.04.2001	6000	18400
29.05.2006	300	1200
10 03 2016	500	3400
Total	6800	23000
disposal	(4000)	(14289)
	2800	8711

Total gain on sale

	£
First match acquisition with 30 days	
Proceeds 500/4000 × 36200	4525
Cost	(3400)
Gain	(1125)
3500/4000 × 36200	31675
Cost 3500/6800 × 19600	(10880)
Gain	20786
Total Gain	21911

Task 11

(1) Desmond bought a house in Glasgow on 1 April 2001. He lived in the house until 30 September 2004. He was then sent to work in Bristol by his employer, before returning to live in the house again on 1 October 2009. He lived in the house before moving out on 30 April 2010 to live with friends until the house was sold on 30 September 2015. *14y 6m · ownership*

Using the proforma layout provided, show which periods of ownership are exempt and which are chargeable matching the correct explanation for each period.

Picklist for explanation:	Picklist for dates:
Not occupied and not followed by actual occupation	1 October 2004 to 30 September 2008 ✓
Actual occupation ✓ *exempt*	1 May 2010 to 31 March 2014
Actual occupation *exempt*	1 April 2001 to 30 September 2004 ✓
Last 18 months ownership *exempt*	1 October 2008 to 30 September 2009 ✓
Up to three years any reason ✓ *exempt*	1 April 2014 to 30 September 2015 ✓
Four years employed elsewhere in UK ✓ *exempt*	1 October 2009 to 30 April 2010 ✓

Explanation	Exempt (dates)	Chargeable (dates)
Actual occupation	*1.04.01 – 30.09.2001*	
4 years employed elsewhere	*1.10.04 – 30.09.2002*	
Up to 3 years any reason	*1.10.08 – 30.09.09*	
Actual occupation	*01.10.09 – 30.04.10*	
Not occupied	*1.05.10 – 31.03.14*	*01.05.10 – 31.03.14*
Last 18 months	*1.04.2014 – 30.09.15*	

(2) Desmond purchased the property for £210,000 on 1 April 2001, and received disposal proceeds of £385,000 on 30 September 2015. It is his main residence.

After applying principle private residence relief, the sale of Desmond's house will result in a chargeable gain.

True ✓

False ☐

(3) **If any capital gains tax is payable on the sale of his house, by what date must Desmond pay this? (xx/xx/xxxx)**

31/01/2017

··

BPP PRACTICE ASSESSMENT 3
PERSONAL TAX

ANSWERS

Task 1

(1) The cost of the car in the taxable benefit computation is:

£21,000	
£22,000	✓
£17,500	
£18,500	

List price £27,000 less capital contribution paid by employee (max) £5,000

(2) The percentage used in the taxable benefit computation is:

30	%

160 – 95 = 65

65 ÷ 5 = 13%

14% + 13% + 3% (diesel) = 30%

(3) The taxable benefit in respect of the provision of fuel for private use is:

£	5,525

£22,100 × 30% × 10/12 (There is no reduction for part reimbursement of private fuel).

Task 2

(a)

(1)

£	236

£10,500 × 3% × 9/12

(2)

£	100

(3)

£	1,575

£3,150 × 6/12

(4)

£	149

£594 × 3/12

(b)

Benefit	Partly exempt	Wholly exempt
Staff party costing £125 per head		✓
Childcare vouchers of £55 per week		✓
Removal expenses of £10,000	✓ (up to £8,000)	
Work related training costing £1,500		✓

(c)

	✓
£6,750 taxable benefit	
£1,000 taxable benefit	✓
No taxable benefit or allowable deduction	
£1,000 allowable deduction	

	£
Amount reimbursed 15,000 × 45p	6,750
Less statutory allowance	
10,000 miles × 45p	(4,500)
5,000 miles × 25p	(1,250)
Taxable benefit	1,000

Task 3

(a)

(1) The rental income taxable for 2015/16 is:

£	5,400

Rental income accrued 2015/16:

1 July 2015 to 31 March 2016 (working in whole months)

9 months × £600 per month

The actual date of receipt of the rent due on 31 March 2016 is not relevant.

(2) The insurance premium allowable as an expense for 2015/16 is:

£	300

£400 × 9/12

(b)

	Flat A £	Flat B £
Income: £500 × 12/ £650 × 8	6,000	5,200
Expenses:		
Council tax	(1,000)	(800)
Water rates	(300)	(300)
Insurance	(350)	(250)
Wear and tear £(5,200 – 800 – 300) = £4,100 × 10%	(0)	(410)
Net income from property	4,350	3,440
Total property income £(4,350 + 3,440)	7,790	
Less loss b/f	(1,200)	
Taxable property income	6,590	

(c)

	✓
Blue Cottage only	
Green Cottage only	
Both Blue Cottage and Green Cottage	
Neither Blue Cottage nor Green Cottage	✓

The accommodation must be available for letting to the public as holiday accommodation for at least 210 days in the tax year (Blue Cottage fails this test) and actually let for at least 105 days during the same tax year (Green Cottage fails this test).

Tutorial note

It is possible to aggregate the periods of actual letting to give an average period for each property in order to satisfy the 105 day test, but this is not relevant here because the aggregate period is less than 210 days. The availability for letting condition must be satisfied independently for each property.

Task 4

(a)

Received net	Received gross
Loan stock from company	Government loan stock ('gilts')
Building society fixed rate bond	
Bank deposit account	

(b)

Source of income	Chargeable	Exempt
Individual Savings Account interest		✓
Government stock interest	✓	
Dividends received from an Individual Savings Account		✓
Bank deposit account interest	✓	

Task 5

(a)

Item	Taxable	Not taxable
Salary	✓	
Tips	✓	
Employer's pension contribution		✓
Reimbursement of business expenses		✓

(b)

	Non-savings income £	Savings income £	Dividend income £	Total £
Employment income	96,870			
Bank interest £1,600 × 100/80		2,000		
Dividends £6,750 × 100/90			7,500	
Net income	96,870	2,000	7,500	106,370
Less: personal allowance	(7,665)			(7,665)
Taxable income	89,205	2,000	7,500	98,705

Workings

	£
Personal allowance	10,600
Less half excess (see below)	(2,935)
	7,665
Total net income	106,370
Adjustment for Gift Aid donation £400 × 100/80	(500)
Adjusted net income	105,870
Less income limit	(100,000)
Excess	5,870

Task 6

(a)

	Non savings income	Savings income	Dividend income
	£	£	£
Employment income	11,250		
Building society interest (£37,000 × 100/80)		46,250	
Dividends (£12,500 × 100/90)			13,889
Personal allowance	(10,600)		
Taxable income	650	46,250	13,889
Income tax			
£650 × 20%			130
£4,350 (£5,000 – £650) × 0%			0
£26,785 (£31,785 – £5,000) × 20%			5,357
£15,115 (£46,250 – £26,785 – £4,350) × 40%			6,046
£13,889 × 32.5%			4,514
Income tax liability			16,047
Less tax credit on dividend (13,889 × 10%)			(1,389)
Less tax deducted at source:			
Building society interest (£46,250 × 20%)			(9,250)
PAYE			(250)
Income tax payable			5,158

(b)

Guy's employer will deduct the donation from his salary before it is taxed. If he decides to pay £50 a month, this will mean he will get tax relief during the year on £600 (£50 × 12). This will reduce his taxable employment income to £50 and his tax liability by £360 as follows:

Income tax			
£50 × 20%			10
£4,950 (£5,000 − £50) × 0%			0
£26,785 (£31,785 − £5,000) × 20%			5,357
£14,515 (£46,250 − £26,785 − £4,950) × 40%			5,806
£13,889 × 32.5%			4,514
Income tax liability			15,687

£16,047 − £15,687 = £360

Task 7

(a)

All records until 31 January 2018	
Employment record until 31 January 2018, interest record until 31 January 2022	
Employment record until 31 January 2022, interest record until 31 January 2018	
All records until 31 January 2022	

(b)

From:	AATStudent@boxmail.net
To:	Raman99@sherbet.net
Sent:	22 June 2016
Subject:	More information

Although you have made an error in your tax return, there is no loss of tax to HMRC reasons I will explain below. Therefore no penalty is chargeable. However, you will need to inform HMRC by amending your tax return.

With regards to the £3,000 pension payment, you are entitled to further tax relief. gross payment is £3,000 × 100/80 = £3,750 because you are treated as making payment net of 20% tax.

As you are a higher rate taxpayer, you are entitled to additional tax relief on this amou The basic rate band of £31,785 is extended by £3,750, so that the 40% tax rate will start until the first £35,535 has been taxed at the basic rates. This will therefore reduce amount of tax you need to pay by £750 (£3,750 × (40% - 20%)).

Task 8

Box 1	Kara Allen
Box 3	15000.00 (2,000 + 13,000)
Box 6	500.00
Box 7	3400.00
Box 10	4300.00
Box 18	1
Box 19	10000.00
Box 20	8000.00
Box 21	2000.00
Box 24	1
Box 25	15500.00
Box 26	16000.00
Box 27	0
Box 30	1
Box 31	17000.00
Box 32	4000.00
Box 33	13000.00

Task 9

(a)

Disposal	Market value used	Actual proceeds used	No gain/no loss disposal
Olivia sells shares for £5,000 to her wife Lucy when they are worth £4,000			✓
William sells land to his brother for £10,000 when it is worth £50,000	✓		
Zeta gives an asset worth £4,000 to her friend Tanya	✓		
Olwyn sells listed shares for proceeds of £12,000		✓	

(b)

The chargeable gain on sale is:

£	11,150

	£
Proceeds of sale	45,000
Less disposal costs £(900 + 350)	(1,250)
Net proceeds of sale	43,750
Less costs of acquisition £(32,000 + 600)	(32,600)
enhancement expenditure	
(not reflected in value of property on disposal)	(Nil)
Chargeable gain	11,150

(c)

(1) The allowable loss on sale is:

	✓
£3,750	✓
£3,500	
£7,000	
£7,250	

	£
Deemed proceeds of sale	6,000
Less disposal costs (10% × £2,500)	(250)
Net proceeds of sale	5,750
Less cost	(9,500)
Allowable loss	(3,750)

(2) True ☐

False ✓

A chattel with a useful life of 50 years or less is a wasting chattel.

Task 10

Share pool

	No of shares	Cost £
14.4.01 Acquisition	6,000	18,400
29.5.06 Rights 1 for 20 × £4 (1/20 × 6,000)	300	1,200
	6,300	19,600
23.2.16 Disposal (3,500/6,300 × £19,600)	(3,500)	(10,889)
c/f	2,800	8,711

Total gain on sale

	£
First match with acquisitions in the next 30 days:	
Proceeds of sale $\dfrac{500}{4,000}$ × £36,200	4,525
Less allowable cost	(3,400)
Gain	1,125
Next match with shares in the share pool:	
Proceeds of sale $\dfrac{3,500}{4,000}$ × £36,200	31,675
Less allowable cost (from share pool above)	(10,889)
Gain	20,786
Total gains (£1,125 + £20,786)	21,911

245

Task 11

(1)

Explanation	Exempt	Chargeable
Actual occupation	1 April 2001 to 30 September 2004	
Four years employed elsewhere in UK	1 October 2004 to 30 September 2008	
Up to three years any reason	1 October 2008 to 30 September 2009	
Actual occupation	1 October 2009 to 30 April 2010	
Not occupied and not followed by actual occupation		1 May 2010 to 31 March 2014
Last 18 months ownership	1 April 2014 to 30 September 2015	

(2) After applying principle private residence relief, the sale of Desmond's house will result in a chargeable gain.

True   ☑

False   ☐

(3) Capital gains tax for 2015/16 is payable by:

31/01/2017

BPP PRACTICE ASSESSMENT 4
PERSONAL TAX

Time allowed: 2 hours

TAXATION DATA

Taxation tables for personal tax – 2015/16

Note that 'TAXATION DATA 1' and 'TAXATION DATA 2' shown below will be available as pop-up windows throughout your live assessment.

TAXATION DATA 1

Pop-up 1

Tax rates and bands

	%	£
Basic rate	20	first 31,785
Higher rate	40	to 150,000
Additional rate	45	over 150,000

Savings income is taxed at 0%, 20%, 40% and 45%.

(0% applies to a maximum of £5,000 of savings income only where non-savings income is below this limit)

Dividends are taxed at 10%, 32.5% and 37.5%.

Personal allowances

	£
Personal allowance for individuals born after 5 April 1938	10,600
Age allowance for individuals born before 6 April 1938	10,660
Income limit for age allowance	27,700

TAXATION DATA 2

Pop-up 2

Car benefit percentage

Emission rating for petrol engines	%
0g/km to 50g/km	5
51g/km to 75g/km	9
76g/km to 94g/km	13
95g/km or more	14% + 1% for every extra 5g/km above 95g/km

Diesel engines – additional 3%

The figure for fuel is £22,100

Authorised mileage rates

First 10,000 miles	45p
Over 10,000 miles	25p

Van scale charge

	£
Charge	3,150
Private fuel provided	594
Low emission van charge	630

HMRC official rate

HMRC official rate	3%

Capital gains tax

Annual exempt amount	£11,100
Tax rate	18%
Higher rate	28%

Task 1

In October 2014 her employer provided Antonia with a secondhand Ford Escort car. It cost the company £14,000, but the list price of this car when bought new was £21,000. The car has a CO_2 emission of 90g/km, and has a petrol engine. The company sold the Ford Escort on 31 December 2015 and immediately provided Antonia with a brand new Volvo car. The Volvo has a list price of £27,000, but Antonia had to make a capital contribution of £6,500 towards it. The car has a CO_2 emission of 180g/km and has a diesel engine.

The company pays for all running costs for both cars including the fuel. Antonia pays £80 per month to the company as part of the cost of fuel used privately.

9 m. Ford
3 m.

(1) **The cost of the Ford Escort in the taxable benefit computation is:**

£ 21000

(2) **The taxable benefit in respect of the provision of the Ford Escort for private use in 2015/16 is:**

£ 2048

(3) **The taxable benefit in respect of the provision of fuel for the Ford Escort for private use in 2015/16 is:**

£ 2155

(4) **The cost of the Volvo in the taxable benefit computation is:**

£ 22000

(5) **The taxable benefit in respect of the provision of the Volvo for private use in 2015/16 is:**

34%

£ 1870

(6) **The taxable benefit in respect of the provision of fuel for the Volvo for private use in 2015/16 is:**

£ 1879

Task 2

(a) Elizabeth's employer provided her with a television for her private use on 6 April 2015, costing £2,500. Elizabeth did not pay anything for the use of the TV.

(1) **The taxable benefit for 2015/16 is:**

£ _500_

Elizabeth buys the TV from her employer for £750 on 5 April 2016, when it is worth £1,875.

(2) **The taxable benefit for 2015/16 is:**

£ _1250_

(b) **Indicate whether the following benefits would be taxable or exempt if provided in 2015/16, by ticking the boxes:**

Item	Taxable	Exempt
Provision of second mobile phone	✓	
Removal costs of £7,500		✓
Provision of parking space at work		✓
Accommodation provided to a caretaker for proper performance of his employment duties		✓
Membership of fitness club	✓	

Task 3

(a) **Is the following statement True or false?**

Property income for a tax year is calculated by taking rental income accrued in the tax year less expenses paid in the tax year.

True ☐ *accrued*

False ☑

(b) Zhu Liu bought an apartment on 1 October 2015. He let it out, unfurnished, from 1 December 2015 at an annual rent of £18,000 payable quarterly in advance. He incurred the following expenses in relation to the property:

	£
General repairs and maintenance, all incurred prior to 5 April 2016	750
Insurance for the 12 month period ended 30 September 2016	300
Decorating paid for on 31 March 2016, for work carried out on 10 April 2016	500
Installing a shower	1,500

Using the proforma layout provided, calculate the property income for 2015/16. Fill in all the unshaded boxes. If an expense is not allowable, enter 0. Both brackets and minus signs can be used to show negative numbers.

	£
Rental income	6000
Repairs	(750)
Insurance	(150)
Decorating	(500) 0
Shower	0
Property income	5100

(c) Hero lets out a room in her main residence throughout 2015/16. The tenant pays her £50 per week. Hero estimates that she incurs extra costs of £9 per week in relation to the letting. Hero has not made any elections in relation to the letting.

Hero's taxable property income profit/(loss) for 2015/16 is:

2600
(468)

	✓
£2,132	
£0	✓
£(468)	
£(1,650)	

Task 4

(a) Using the proforma layout provided, show whether the following amounts of interest are received net of basic rate tax or gross by an individual taxpayer:

Building society interest *net*
Bank interest *net*
Government stock interest *gross*
Company loan stock interest *net*

Received net	Received gross

(b) Myrtle was born in 1923, and has the following income for 2015/16: pension income of £18,000, bank interest of £4,800 and dividends of £3,600.

6000   *4000*

(1) **Myrtle's net income for 2015/16 is:**

£ *28000*

(2) **The age allowance that Myrtle is entitled to for 2015/16 is:**

£ *10600*

....

Task 5

(a) Millie is employed by RST plc. For each of the following payments, state the amount of employment income taxable in 2015/16. If an amount is not taxable in 2015/16 enter 0.

(1) Monthly salary of £2,000. Millie becomes entitled to each month's salary on the 25th of each month and it is paid to her on the 28th of each month. Due to a bank error, the salary for March 2015 was not paid to her until 10 April 2015.

The employment income for 2015/16 is:

£ *24000*

(2) Commission of £1,200 paid with her April 2016 salary. The commission relates to sales made in the month of March 2016.

The employment income for 2015/16 is:

£ *0*

(3) Bonus of £5,000 paid on 30 April 2015 based on company's accounting profit for the year ended 31 December 2014.

The employment income for 2015/16 is:

£ | 5000

(4) Reimbursement of business expenses of £500 in December 2014. There is a dispensation in force for such payments with HMRC.

The employment income for 2015/16 is:

£ | 0

(b) In 2015/16, Calum had the following income:

Salary   £47,900
Building society interest   £144    180
Dividends   £90   100

Calum made a contribution of £2,500 to his employer's occupational pension scheme.

Using the proforma layout provided, prepare a computation of taxable income for 2015/16, clearly showing the distinction between the different types of income. Both brackets and minus signs can be used to show negative numbers.

	Non-savings income £	Savings income £	Dividend income £	Total £
Salary	47900			
less P. contr.	2500			
Emp. income	45400			
Interest		180		
Dividends			100	
	45400	180	100	45680
less PA	(10600)			(10600)
Taxable income	34800	180	100	35080

Task 6

(a) Ian had has the following amounts of taxable income (AFTER deduction of his personal allowance) for 2015/16:

	£
Non-savings income	38,382
Savings income	180 ~~225~~
Dividend income	400 ~~144~~

Ian paid £100 to Oxfam in November 2015 and made a Gift Aid declaration.

Ian's tax liability on each source of income for 2015/16 is as follows:

(1) **Non-savings income:**

£ | 8571 | ~~25 49~~ = 29+6

(2) **Savings income:**

£ | 72 |

(3) **Dividend income:**

£ | 130 |

Handwritten working:
31 785 × 20% = 6357
125 × 20% = 25
6472 √ 40% 2589

(b)

(1) Max earns £2,500 in 2015/16 in a part-time job. He also has property income of £15,000 in 2015/16 from letting out a field.

The maximum personal pension contribution on which Max can get tax relief in 2015/16 is:

	✓
£2,500	
£3,600	✓
£7,500	
£5,000	

(2) **Max's tax liability for 2015/16 is:**

£ | 1380 |

Task 7

(a) A client has told you that she forgot to include some bank interest in the tax return you prepared and she does not intend to tell HMRC of the omission.

What TWO actions should you take?

	✓
Inform the Association of Accounting Technicians about the omission	
Report the client's refusal and the facts surrounding it to your firm's Money Laundering Reporting Officer	√
Inform the client in writing that it is not possible for you to act for her in connection with that return	√
Inform HMRC about the omission	

(b)

1 Horse Lane
Trotter Village
Westhampton
WW44 1EE

28 November 2015

Dear Accountant

Please find enclosed all the information that I think you will need to complete my tax return for 2015/16.

However, I have never had to complete a tax return before, and as the tax year ended some months ago, I am a little concerned that I may have missed a crucial deadline.

Please advise me when my return is due and if I will incur any penalties. Also I would like to know when I need to pay any tax that I owe.

Regards

Mahmood

Write notes for inclusion in your reply to Mahmood's letter.

Task 8

You act for Saul Bentner. He owns two properties and has given you the following information:

	Property A £	Property B £
Annual income:		
Rent	6,000	4,000
Annual expenses:		
Redecoration	1,000	800
Cleaning	300	n/a
Insurance	350	250
Letting agent's fees	1,500	400

Property A is let furnished. Property B is let unfurnished.

Using this information complete the property income pages of Saul's tax return.

UK property

Tax year 6 April 2015 to 5 April 2016

Your name

S a u l   b e n t n e r

Your Unique Taxpayer Reference (UTR)

UK property details

1 Number of properties rented out

2

2 If all property income ceased in 2015–16 and you do not expect to receive such income in 2016–17, put 'X' in the box and consider if you need to complete the *Capital gains summary* page

3 If you have any income from property let jointly, put 'X' in the box

4 If you are claiming Rent a Room relief and your rents are £4,250 or less nor £2,125 if let jointly), put 'X' in the box

Furnished holiday lettings (FHL) in the UK or European Economic Area (EEA)

Fill in one page for UK businesses and a separate page for EEA businesses. Please read the *UK property notes* before filling in boxes 5 to 19 if you have furnished holiday lettings

5 Income – *the amount of rent and any income for services provided to tenants*

£ · 0 0

6 Rent paid, repairs, insurance and costs of services provided – *the total amount*

£ · 0 0

7 Loan interest and other financial cost

£ · 0 0

8 Legal, management and other professional fee

£ · 0 0

9 Other allowable property expenses

£ · 0 0

10 Private use adjustment – *if expenses include any amounts for non-business purposes*

£ · 0 0

11 Balancing charges – *read the notes*

£ · 0 0

12 Capital allowances – *read the notes*

£ · 0 0

13 Adjusted profit for the year (if the amount in box 5 + box 10 + box 11 minus (boxes 6 to 9 + box 12) is positive)

£ · 0 0

14 Loss brought forward used against this year's profit – *if you have a non-FHL property business loss read the notes on property losses*

£ · 0 0

15 Taxable profit for the year (box 13 minus box 14)

£ · 0 0

16 Loss for the year (if the amount in boxes 6 to 9 + box 12 minus (box 5 + box 10 + box 11) is positive)

£ · 0 0

17 Total loss to carry forward

£ · 0 0

18 If this business is in the EEA, put 'X' in the box – *read the notes*

19 If you want to make a period of grace election, put 'X' in the box

SA105 2014   Page UKP 1   HMRC 12/14
5013441

259

Property income

Do not include furnished holiday lettings, Real Estate Investment Trust or Property Authorised Investment Funds dividends/distributions here.

20 Total rents and other income from property

£ 1 0 0 0 0 · 0 0

21 Tax taken off any income in box 20

£ · 0 0

22 Premiums for the grant of a lease – from box E on the Working Sheet – *read the notes*

£ · 0 0

23 Reverse premiums and inducements

£ · 0 0

Property expenses

24 Rent, rates, insurance, ground rents etc

£ 6 0 0 · 0 0

25 Property repairs, maintenance and renewals

£ 1 8 0 0 · 0 0

26 Loan interest and other financial cost

£ · 0 0

27 Legal, management and other professional fee

£ 1 9 0 0 · 0 0

28 Costs of services provided, including wages

£ 5 0 0 · 0 0

29 Other allowable property expenses

£ 1 0 0 · 0 0

Calculating your taxable profit or loss

30 Private use adjustment – *read the notes*

£ · 0 0

31 Balancing charges – *read the notes*

£ · 0 0

32 Annual Investment Allowance

£ · 0 0

33 Business Premises Renovation Allowance (Assisted Areas only) – *read the notes*

£ · 0 0

34 All other capital allowances

£ · 0 0

35 Landlord's Energy Saving Allowance

£ · 0 0

36 10% wear and tear allowance – *for furnished residential accommodation only*

£ 6 0 0 · 0 0

37 Rent a Room exempt amount

£ · 0 0

38 Adjusted profit for the year – from box O on the Working Sheet – *read the notes*

£ 4 8 0 0 · 0 0

39 Loss brought forward used against this year's profit

£ 0 · 0 0

40 Taxable profit for the year (box 38 minus box 39

£ 4 8 0 0 · 0 0

41 Adjusted loss for the year – from box O on the Working Sheet – *read the notes*

£ · 0 0

42 Loss set off against 2015–16 total income – *this will be unusual – read the notes*

£ · 0 0

43 Loss to carry forward to following year, including unused losses brought forward

£ · 0 0

Task 9

(a) **Classify whether a disposal of each of the following assets will be chargeable to or exempt from capital gains tax:**

Asset	Chargeable	Exempt
Plot of land sold for £20,000	✓	☐
Diamond brooch sold for £3,500 which cost £2,000	☐	✓
Shares in an unlisted company sold for £10,000	✓	☐
1930 Rolls Royce car sold for £100,000	☐	✓

(b) Jaycee made the following gains and loss in 2015/16:

	£
Gain on shares September 2015	18,500
Gain on painting December 2015	6,000
Gain on house January 2016 (not her PPR)	18,895
Loss on vase April 2015	(10,000)

Jaycee is a higher rate taxpayer.

(1) **Her capital gains tax liability for 2015/16 is:**

£   6243

(2) **The due date for payment of this liability is: (enter date as xx/xx/xxxx)**

31/01/17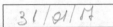

(c) In December 2015, Mabel gave her son an asset worth £20,000. She had acquired the asset for £25,000.

In March 2016, Mabel gave her sister an asset worth £30,000. Mable had acquired the asset for £22,000.

Mabel's chargeable gains (before the annual exempt amount) for 2015/16 are:

£   8000

Task 10

Ming Lee bought 1,000 shares in Lavender Ltd for £5,000 in October 2005. In May 2007, she received 200 shares in a bonus issue. In January 2011 the company offered a rights issue at 1 share for every 6 held. She accepted this rights issue at £3 per share. She sold 1,000 shares in Lavender Ltd in January 2016 for £12,400.

Clearly showing the balance of shares and their value to carry forward, calculate the chargeable gain on sale of the shares. All workings must be shown.

10/2005	1000	5000
05/07	200	0
01/11	200	600
	1400	5600
Disposal	(1000)	(4000)
	400	1600
Proceeds	12,400	
Cost	(4000)	
Gain	8400	

Task 11

(a) On 1 March 1995, Craig bought a house for £36,000. He had lived in it until 1 September 1998, when he went to Australia to take up employment. He returned from there on 1 September 2004 and moved back into the house until 1 February 2010 when he purchased a small flat. He has lived in the flat since then. Craig finally sold the house for £178,000 on 31 October 2015.   *20 y. 8m. ownership*

Using the proforma layout below, show the chargeable gain on sale. Both brackets and minus signs can be used to show negative numbers.

Chargeable gain on sale of property	£
Proceeds of sale	178 000
Less allowable cost	(36 000)
Gain before PPR	142 000
Less PPR exempt amount	(112 798)
Chargeable gain	29 202

(b) During 2015/16 Nina has sold an asset giving rise to a chargeable gain of £20,100. She has capital losses brought forward at 6 April 2015 of £11,000.

The amount of capital losses Nina will have to carry forward at 5 April 2016 is

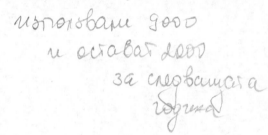

	✓
£2,000	✓
£0	
£11,000	
£9,000	

BPP
LEARNING MEDIA

BPP PRACTICE ASSESSMENT 4
PERSONAL TAX

ANSWERS

Task 1

(1) The cost of the Ford Escort in the taxable benefit computation is:

£	21,000

(2) The taxable benefit in respect of the provision of the Ford Escort for private use in 2015/16 is:

£	2,048

£21,000 × 13% (CO_2 emissions of 90g/km) × 9/12

(3) The taxable benefit in respect of the provision of fuel for the Ford Escort for private use in 2015/16 is:

£	2,155

£22,100 × 13% × 9/12 (no reduction for partial reimbursement of private fuel)

(4) The cost of the Volvo in the taxable benefit computation is:

£	22,000

£27,000 – £5,000 (max deduction for capital contribution)

(5) The taxable benefit in respect of the provision of the Volvo for private use in 2015/16 is:

£	1,870

£22,000 × 34% × 3/12

180 – 95 = 85

85 ÷ 5 = 17%

14% + 17% + 3% (diesel) = 34%

(6) The taxable benefit in respect of the provision of fuel for the Volvo for private use in 2015/16 is:

£	1,879

£22,100 × 34% × 3/12 (no reduction for partial reimbursement of private fuel)

Task 2

(a)

(1) The taxable benefit for 2015/16 is:

£	500

Use of asset £2,500 × 20%

(2) The taxable benefit for 2015/16 is:

£	1,250

Greater of:

		£
(i)	Original market value	2,500
	Less assessed for use 2015/16	(500)
		2,000
(ii)	Market value at acquisition by employee	1,875

Greater = £2,000 less amount paid by Elizabeth of £750

(b)

Item	Taxable	Exempt
Provision of second mobile phone	✓	
Removal costs of £7,500		✓
Provision of parking space at work		✓
Accommodation provided to a caretaker for proper performance of his employment duties		✓
Membership of fitness club	✓	

Task 3

(a)

True ☐

False ☑

Property income for a tax year is calculated by taking rental income accrued in the tax year less expenses accrued in the tax year.

(b)

	£
Rental income £18,000 × 4/12	6,000
Repairs	(750)
Insurance £300 × 6/12	(150)
Decorating (not accrued in 2014/15)	0
Shower (capital expense)	0
Property income	5,100

(c) Hero's taxable property income profit/(loss) for 2015/16 is

	✓
£2,132	
£0	✓
£(468)	
£(1,650)	

Hero has no taxable property income profit for 2015/16 because the income from the letting is £50 × 52 = £2,600, which is less than the rent a room limit. Rent a room relief applies automatically when rental income is below £4,250, unless the taxpayer makes an election to use the usual property income rules.

Task 4

(a)

Received net	Received gross
Building society interest	Government stock interest
Bank interest	
Company loan stock interest	

(b)

(1) Myrtle's net income for 2015/16 is:

£ | 28,000

	Non-savings income £	Savings income £	Dividend income £	Total £
Pension income	18,000			
Bank interest (× 100/80)		6,000		
Dividends (× 100/90)			4,000	
Net income	18,000	6,000	4,000	28,000

(2) The age allowance that Myrtle is entitled to for 2015/16 is:

£ | 10,600

	£
Total net income	28,000
Less income limit	(27,700)
Excess	300
Age allowance	10,660
Less half excess	(150)
	10,510
Minimum allowance	10,600

Task 5

(a)

(1) The employment income for 2015/16 is:

£ | 24,000

April 2015 to March 2016 = 12 × £2,000

The salary for March 2015 was received for tax purposes on 25 March 2015 when Millie became entitled to it and so was taxed in 2014/15.

---

(2) The employment income for 2015/16 is:

£ | 0

Commission received 25 April 2016 (taxed in 2016/17)

(3) The employment income for 2015/16 is:

£ | 5,000

Bonus received 30 April 2015

(4) The employment income for 2015/16 is:

£ | 0

Reimbursement with dispensation (ignored)

(b)

	Non-savings income £	Savings income £	Dividend income £	Total £
Employment income:				
Salary	47,900			
Less occupational pension contribution	(2,500)			
Employment income	45,400			
Building society interest (× 100/80)		180		
Dividends (× 100/90)			100	
Net income	45,400	180	100	45,680
Less personal allowance	(10,600)			(10,600)
Taxable income	34,800	180	100	35,080

Task 6

(a)

(1) Non-savings income:

£	8,971

	£
£31,785 × 20%	6,357
£125 (£100 × 100/80) × 20% (extended band)	25
£6,472 × 40% (£38,382 - £31,785 - £125)	2,589
	8,971

(2) Savings income:

£	72

£180 × 40%

(3) Dividend income:

£	130

£400 × 32.5%

(b)

(1) The maximum pension contribution on which Max can get tax relief in 2015/16 is:

	✓
£2,500	
£3,600	✓
£7,500	
£5,000	

Higher of earnings and £3,600. Property income is not earnings unless it is from qualifying holiday accommodation.

(2) Max's tax liability for 2015/16 is:

£	1,380

Total income is £2,500 + £15,000 = £17,500

Less PA of £10,600 = £6,900 (Taxable non-savings income)

Income tax is £6,900 × 20% = £1,380

Task 7

(a)

	✓
Inform the Association of Accounting Technicians about the omission	
Report the client's refusal and the facts surrounding it to your firm's Money Laundering Reporting Officer	✓
Inform the client in writing that it is not possible for you to act for her in connection with that return	✓
Inform HMRC about the omission	

(b) There are two key dates for when tax returns are due:

For paper based version of the tax return it is 31 October 2016 (now passed)

For electronic based version of the tax return it is 31 January 2017

Provided that the return is completed online by 31 January 2017 no penalty will be payable. The tax liability will automatically be calculated on completion of the online return.

If you owe any tax this will be due on the same date. Also you may then need to make interim payments for 2016/17. The first of these will also be due on 31 January 2017 and will be calculated as half of the amount of tax due by self assessment for 2015/16.

Task 8

Your name:	Saul Bentner
Box 1	2
Box 20	10000.00
Box 24	600.00
Box 25	1800.00
Box 27	1900.00
Box 28	300.00
Box 36	600.00
Box 38	4800.00
Box 40	4800.00

Task 9

(a)

Asset	Chargeable	Exempt
Plot of land sold for £20,000	✓	
Diamond brooch sold for £3,500 which cost £2,000		✓ (cost and proceeds more than £6,000
Shares in an unlisted company sold for £10,000	✓	
1930 Rolls Royce car sold for £100,000		✓ (all cars exempt)

(b)

(1) Her capital gains tax liability for 2015/16 is:

£	6,243

	£
Gain on shares	18,500
Gain on painting	6,000
Gain on house	18,895
Chargeable gains	43,395
Less allowable loss on vase	(10,000)
Net chargeable gains for year	33,395
Less annual exempt amount	(11,100)
Taxable gains	22,295
CGT £22,295 × 28%	6,243

(2) The due date for payment of this liability is:

31/01/2017

(c) Mabel's chargeable gains (before the annual exempt amount) for 2015/16 are:

£	8,000

	£
Gift to her sister:	
Deemed proceeds of sale (market value)	30,000
Less allowable cost	(22,000)
Chargeable gain	8,000

Both the son and the sister are connected persons for Mabel. However, the loss of £5,000 on the disposal to the son can only be set against gains made to him, not to another connected person.

Task 10

Share pool

	No of shares	Cost
		£
October 2005 Acquisition	1,000	5,000
May 2007 Bonus	200	Nil
	1,200	5,000
January 2011 Rights 1 for 6 × £3		
(1/6 × 1,200 = 200 shares × £3 = £600)	200	600
	1,400	5,600
January 2016 Disposal		
(1,000/1,400 × £5,600)	(1,000)	(4,000)
c/f	400	1,600
Gain		
Proceeds of sale		12,400
Less allowable cost		(4,000)
Chargeable gain		8,400

Task 11

(a)

Chargeable gain on sale of property	£
Proceeds of sale	178,000
Less allowable cost	(36,000)
Gain before PPR	142,000
Less PPR exempt amount (W) £142,000 × 197/248	(112,798)
Chargeable gain	29,202

Working

Time period	Chargeable months	Exempt months	Total months
1.3.95 to 31.8.98		42	42
1.9.98 to 31.8.04 (Note 1)		72	72
1.9.04 to 31.1.10		65	65
1.2.10 to 31.10.15 (Note 2)	51	18	69
	51	197	248

Notes

1   Any period of employment abroad is treated as deemed occupation if it is preceded and followed by actual occupation.

2   Last 18 months of ownership is always exempt if the property has been the taxpayer's only or main residence at some time during the ownership period.

(b)   The amount of capital losses Nina will have to carry forward at 5 April 2016 is

£2,000	✓
£0	
£11,000	
£9,000	

The capital loss brought forward will be used to bring the chargeable gain for 2015/16 to the level of the annual exempt amount. This uses £9,000 of the loss leaving £2,000 to carry forward to 2016/17.

BPP PRACTICE ASSESSMENT 5
PERSONAL TAX

Time allowed: 2 hours

TAXATION DATA

Taxation tables for personal tax – 2015/16

Note that 'TAXATION DATA 1' and 'TAXATION DATA 2' shown below will be available as pop-up windows throughout your live assessment.

TAXATION DATA 1

Pop-up 1

Tax rates and bands

	%	£
Basic rate	20	first 31,785
Higher rate	40	to 150,000
Additional rate	45	over 150,000

Savings income is taxed at 0%, 20%, 40% and 45%.

(0% applies to a maximum of £5,000 of savings income only where non-savings income is below this limit)

Dividends are taxed at 10%, 32.5% and 37.5%.

Personal allowances

	£
Personal allowance for individuals born after 5 April 1938	10,600
Age allowance for individuals born before 6 April 1938	10,660
Income limit for age allowance	27,700

TAXATION DATA 2

Pop-up 2

Car benefit percentage

Emission rating for petrol engines	%
0g/km to 50g/km	5
51g/km to 75g/km	9
76g/km to 94g/km	13
95g/km or more	14% + 1% for every extra 5g/km above 95g/km

Diesel engines – additional 3%

The figure for fuel is £22,100

Authorised mileage rates

First 10,000 miles	45p
Over 10,000 miles	25p

Van scale charge

	£
Charge	3,150
Private fuel provided	594
Low emission van charge	630

HMRC official rate
3%

Capital gains tax

Annual exempt amount	£11,100
Tax rate	18%
Higher rate	28%

Task 1

(a) Yan is provided with a company car for business and private use throughout 2015/16. The car had a list price of £17,200 when bought new in December 2014, although the company paid £16,000 for the car after a dealer discount. Yan made a contribution of £2,000 to the cost of the car.

The car has a petrol engine and has CO_2 emissions of 117g/km. The company pays for all running costs, including all fuel. Yan does not make any contribution for his private use of the car.

(1) **The cost of the car in the taxable benefit computation is:**

£  15 200

(2) **The percentage used in the taxable benefit computation is:**

 18 %

(3) **The taxable benefit in respect of the provision of fuel for private use is:**

£ 39 78

(b) You have received the following email from Matt Taylor:

From: MTaylor@boxmail.net
To: AATStudent@boxmail.net
Sent: 14 June 2016 11:35
Subject: Car

I have recently been promoted and now have to do some travelling by car on business, probably about 6,000 miles a year. My employer has given me two options:

(1) A company car with a list price of £15,000. It has a petrol engine. The car is environmentally friendly and so has CO_2 emissions of only 85g/km. I will be able to use the car for both business and private purposes, but I will be required to repay the cost of my private fuel.

(2) A mileage allowance of 35p per business mile if I use my own car.

Can you please explain the taxation aspects of each of the options?

Thanks, Matt

Reply to Matt's email

From:	AATStudent@boxmail.net
To:	MTaylor@boxmail.net
Sent:	16 June 2016 10:41
Subject:	Car

Task 2

(a)

(1) Marge has recently started to work for LMN plc and earns £30,000 a year. She is entitled to childcare vouchers of £60 per week for 45 weeks in 2015/16.

The taxable benefit for 2015/16 is:

£ _225_

(2) **Tick to show if the following statement is True or False.**

The maximum amount of exempt benefit for the additional costs of home working is £4 per week.

True ☐

False ☑

(b) **For each of the following benefits, tick whether they would be wholly or partly taxable or wholly exempt if received in 2015/16:**

Item	Wholly or partly taxable	Wholly exempt
Award of £25 under staff suggestion scheme	☐	☑
Removal expenses of £9,000	☑	☐
Incidental personal expenses of working away from home in the UK of £10 per night	☑	☐
Staff party at cost of £100 per head	☐	☑

(c) Antonia is employed by Zed Ltd. She receives store vouchers from the company as a Christmas bonus in December 2015. These enable her to buy goods worth £300. Her employer bought the vouchers from the store for £267.

(1) **The taxable benefit for 2015/16 is:**

£ _267_

Antonia is also loaned £12,000 by Zed Ltd on 1 July 2015. She pays interest at an annual rate of 0.5% on the loan. She does not make any capital repayments in 2015/16.

(2) **The taxable benefit for 2015/16 is:**

£ _225_

Task 3

(a) Ronnie buys a house on 6 May 2015 and rents it out on 6 August 2015. He charges an annual rent of £9,000, payable in advance. He pays an annual insurance premium on 6 June 2015 of £600.   *£m.*   *10m ins.*

Ronnie's taxable property income for 2015/16 is: 6000 − 500

£	5500

(b) A client, Mohamed Albayouk, has sent in the following information for 2015/16 in relation to his two properties that he rents out.

17 Wool Lane is unfurnished and is rented out at £560 per month. 42 Silk Street is furnished and is rented out at £800 per month. Both properties were occupied throughout 2015/16.

The expenses for the year were: *unf.*   *fur*

Item	17 Wool Lane £	42 Silk Street £
Insurance	300	280
Water rates	160	176
Council tax	1,800	2,100
Cleaning	800	500
Redecoration	1,000	0
Cost of furniture	0	3,450

The wear and tear allowance is claimed where relevant.

Calculate the property income taxable on Mohamed Albayouk for 2015/16 using the proforma layout provided. Fill in all the unshaded boxes. If any item is not an allowable expense, enter 0. Both brackets and minus signs can be used to show negative numbers.

	17 Wool Lane	42 Silk Street
	£	£
Income:		
Rents	6720	9600
Expenses:		
Insurance	(300)	(280)
Water rates	(160)	(176)
Council tax	(1800)	(2100 ·)
Cleaning	(800)	(500)
Redecoration	(1000)	0
Furniture	0	0
Wear and tear	0	(732)
Property income	2660	5812
Total Property income		8472

(c) Asif owns three properties which he lets out throughout 2015/16. He makes a profit of £5,000 on Property 1, a loss of £1,200 on Property 2 and a profit of £2,000 on Property 3. Asif also has a property loss of £1,500 brought forward at 5 April 2015.

The property income taxable on Asif for 2015/16 is:

£ | 4300

Task 4

(a) **During 2015/16, Mimi received the following income. In each case, show the amount of income that she should enter on her tax return. If the income is exempt, enter 0.**

(1) Property income £2,000.

£	2000

(2) Premium bond prize £100.

£	0

(3) Government stock interest £80.

£	80

(4) Dividends received £1,800.

£	2000

(b) Marcello receives a dividend of £5,400 in March 2016.

(1) **The amount of the dividend that Marcello will enter on his tax return is:**

£	6000

(2) **The tax credit attaching to the dividend is:**

£	600

(3) Marcello has no other income.

Is the following statement True or False?

Marcello will receive a repayment of the amount of the tax credit.

True ☐

False ☑

BPP
LEARNING MEDIA

Task 5

Andrea is a director of Z Ltd and provides you with the following information:

(1) Monthly salary of £7,500 paid on 25th day of each month

(2) Bonus A of £17,500 based on company's accounting profit for the period of account ended 31 March 2015, determined on 31 October 2015. Andrea became entitled to be paid this bonus on 30 April 2016 and it was actually paid to her on 30 June 2016.

(3) Bonus B of £22,500 based on company's accounting profit for the period of account ended 31 July 2016, determined on 31 March 2016. Andrea became entitled to be paid this bonus on 30 June 2016 and it was actually paid to her on 30 September 2016.

(4) 5% of basic salary paid into the company pension scheme each tax year, Z Ltd matches these contributions.

(5) Use of a company car which has a taxable benefit for 2015/16 of £3,250. No fuel is provided for private use.

(6) Dividends received of £3,800, and interest of £750 from an ISA.

Complete the following table showing the figures to be included in Andrea's taxable income for 2015/16. Use whole pounds only. If your answer is zero, please insert a '0'. Do not use brackets or minus signs.

	£
Salary	90000
Bonus A	17 500
Bonus B	0
Director's pension contribution	(4500)
Company's pension contribution	0
Company car benefit	3250
Dividends	4222
Interest from ISA	0
Net income	110 472
Personal allowance	(5364)
Taxable income	105 108

Task 6

Andrew, born in 1966, has income as follows:

	£
Employment income	46,000
Bank interest received	1,600 *2000*
Dividends received	4,500 *5000*

Andrew makes a Gift Aid donation of £1,200 in July 2015.

(a) Calculate his total income tax liability for 2015/16, using the table given below. Both brackets and minus signs can be used to show negative numbers.

	£
Employment Income	46000
Interest	2000
Dividends	5000
Net Income	53 000
Less PA	(10 600)
Taxable Income	42 400
31 785 x 20%	6857
1 800 x 20%	800
8115 x 40%	5846
2000 x 40%	800
5000 x 32,5%	1625
Tax liability	19928

(b) On which dates are payment on accounts due for 2015/16?

	✓
31 January 2016 and 31 July 2016	✓
31 January 2017 and 31 July 2017	
31 July 2016 and 31 January 2017	
31 October 2016 and 31 January 2017	

Task 7

(a) You are a sole practitioner and suspect that one of your clients may be engaged in money laundering.

Who should you inform about your suspicions?

	✓
National Crime Agency	√
Association of Taxation Technicians	
Tax Tribunal	
HM Treasury	

(b) On 30 September 2016 your client, Jakki, leaves the following message on your voicemail:

'Hi, it's Jakki. I know that I am a new client to your practice and that you did not prepare my tax return for 2014/15, but I have just discovered that I failed to notify HMRC of some dividends that I received in January 2015. I simply forgot about them, but I am worried that HMRC will find out that I have not paid the right amount of tax on this income. Can you please advise about what I should do and about any penalties that I may incur? Thanks.'

List the information that you need to give Jakki when you ring her back to discuss this issue.

Task 8

You act for Gary Bryant, who works for HGK plc. He has given you the following information about his employment in relation to the tax year 2015/16:

	£
Gross salary	30,000
Occupational pension payment deducted	2,500
Tax taken off pay	4,200
Company car benefit	3,200
Private medical insurance	1,500
Professional subscription paid by Gary	300

Using this information complete the employment income page.

Employment

Tax year 6 April 2015 to 5 April 2016

Your name

Gary Bryant

Your unique taxpayer reference (UTR)

Complete an *Employment* page for each employment or directorship

1 Pay from this employment - the total from your P45 or P60
- *before tax was taken off*

£ 27500 . 0 0

2 UK tax taken off pay in box 1

£ – 4200 . 0 0

3 Tips and other payments not on your P60 - *read page EN 3 of the notes*

£ . 0 0

4 PAYE tax reference of your employer (on your P45/P60)

5 Your employer's name

HGK plc

6 If you were a company director, put 'X' in the box

7 And, if the company was a close company, put 'X' in the box

8 If you are a part-time teacher in England or Wales and are on the Repayment of Teachers' Loans Scheme for this employment, put 'X' in the box

Benefits from your employment - use your form P11D (or equivalent information)

9 Company cars and vans - *the total 'cash equivalent' amount*

£ 3200 . 0 0

10 Fuel for company cars and vans - *the total 'cash equivalent' amount*

£ . 0 0

11 Private medical and dental insurance - *the total 'cash equivalent' amount*

£ 1500 . 0 0

12 Vouchers, credit cards and excess mileage allowance

£ . 0 0

13 Goods and other assets provided by your employer
- *the total value or amount*

£ . 0 0

14 Accommodation provided by your employer - *the total value or amount*

£ . 0 0

15 Other benefits (including interest-free and low interest loans) - *the total 'cash equivalent' amount*

£ . 0 0

16 Expenses payments received and balancing charges

£ . 0 0

Employment expenses

17 Business travel and subsistence expenses

£ . 0 0

18 Fixed deductions for expenses

£ . 0 0

19 Professional fees and subscriptions

£ 300 . 0 0

20 Other expenses and capital allowances

£ . 0 0

Shares schemes, employment lump sums, compensation, deductions and Seafarers' Earnings Deduction are on the *Additional information* pages enclosed in the tax return pack

SA102 2014   Tax return: Employment: Page E 1   HMRC 12/13

Task 9

(a) For each of the following assets, tick whether they are chargeable or exempt assets for capital gains tax:

Asset	Chargeable	Exempt
Horse	☐	☑
Field in which horse is kept	☑	☐
Antique horse brass costing £500, worth £1,700	☐	☑

(b) Ulma bought a holiday cottage for £65,000 and spent £15,000 on an extension and £10,000 on redecoration. She sold the cottage for £125,000 on 10 August 2015.

The chargeable gain on sale is:

£ | 45000

(c) Jade purchased a emerald bracelet for £8,000. She sold the bracelet in August 2015 at auction for £2,700 (which was net of 10% commission).

The allowable loss on sale is:

£ | 2300

6000
(300)
5700
(8000)
2300

Task 10

Merrill paid £5,000 for 2,000 shares in Bug plc in August 2009. In September 2012, there was a one for one bonus issue. Merrill sold 1,000 shares in June 2015 for £8,000.

Compute the chargeable gain and the value of the share pool following the disposal, using the proforma layout provided. Both brackets and minus signs can be used to show negative numbers.

Gain

	£
Proceeds	8000
Cost	(1250)
Gain	6750

Share pool

	No of shares	Cost £
10/09	2000	5000
09/12	2000	0
	4000	5000
06/15	(1000)	(1250)
c/f	3000	3750

Task 11

(a) Jai makes chargeable gains of £15,100 in November 2015. Jai's taxable income for 2015/16 is £31,390 and he made a Gift Aid payment of £400 to Oxfam in May 2015.

   500

   The CGT payable for 2015/16 is:

   £ | 1030

(b) **Tick to show if the following statement is True or False.**

   The last 18 months of ownership of a house are exempt provided that the house is lived in by the owner at some time during that 18 month period.

   True ☐

   False ☑

BPP PRACTICE ASSESSMENT 5
PERSONAL TAX

ANSWERS

Task 1

(a)

(1) The cost of the car in the taxable benefit computation is:

£ | 15,200

List price less capital contribution made by Yan

(2) The percentage used in the taxable benefit computation is:

18 | %

$115 - 95 = 20$

$20 \div 5 = 4\%$

$14\% + 4\%$

(3) The taxable benefit in respect of the provision of fuel for private use is:

£ | 3,978

£22,100 × 18%

(b)

From:	AAT Student@boxmail.net
To:	MTaylor@boxmail.net
Sent:	16 June 2016 10.41
Subject:	Car

The provision of the company car will be a taxable benefit because it is available for private use. The benefit is the list price of the car multiplied by a percentage. In this case, because the car has CO_2 emissions of between 76g/km and 94g/km, the percentage will be 13%. The benefit will therefore be £15,000 × 13% = £1,950 per tax year. There will be no fuel benefit because you will be reimbursing the cost of your private fuel.

There is a statutory mileage allowance which would apply if you use your own car for business purposes. The rate is 45p per mile up to 10,000 miles per year. As your employer would only be paying you 35p per mile, the extra 10p per mile could be claimed by you as an allowable deduction when working out your employment income. If you travelled 6,000 business miles in a tax year, the deduction would be 6,000 × 10p = £600.

Task 2

(a)

(1) The taxable benefit for 2015/16 is:

£	225

£(60 – 55) = £5 × 45

(2) True ☐

    False ☑

Payments in excess of £4 per week can be exempt benefits provided that evidence will be given that the payment is wholly in respect of additional household expenses incurred by the employee in carrying out his duties at home.

(b)

Item	Wholly or partly taxable	Wholly exempt
Award of £25 under staff suggestion scheme		✓
Removal expenses of £9,000	✓ (limit £8,000))	
Incidental personal expenses of working away from home in the UK of £10 per night	✓ (wholly taxable if exceeds £5)	
Staff party at cost of £100 per head		✓ (up to £150

(c)

(1) The taxable benefit for 2015/16 is:

£	267

Cost to employer

(2) The taxable benefit for 2015/16 is:

£	225

£12,000 × (3 – 0.5)% × 9/12

Task 3

(a) Ronnie's taxable property income for 2015/16 is:

£	5,500

	£
Rent accrued £9,000 × 8/12	6,000
Less expense £600 × 10/12	(500)
Property income 2015/16	5,500

Income and expenses are taxed on the accruals basis.

(b)

	17 Wool Lane £	42 Silk Street £
Income:		
Rents £560/800 × 12	6,720	9,600
Expenses:		
Insurance	(300)	(280)
Water rates	(160)	(176)
Council tax	(1,800)	(2,100)
Cleaning	(800)	(500)
Redecoration	(1,000)	0
Furniture	0	0
Wear and tear £(9,600 − 176 − 2,100) × 10%	0	(732)
Property income	2,660	5,812
Total property income	8,472	

(c) The property income taxable on Asif for 2015/16 is:

£	4,300

	£
Property 1 profit	5,000
Property 2 loss	(1,200)
Property 3 profit	2,000
	5,800
Less loss b/f	(1,500)
Property income 2015/16	4,300

Task 4

(a)

(1) Property income £2,000.

£	2,000

(2) Premium bond prize £100.

£	0

Exempt

(3) Government stock interest £80.

£	80

Received gross

(4) Dividends received £1,800

£	2,000

£1,800 × 100/90

(b)

(1) The amount of the dividend that Marcello will enter on his tax return is:

£	6,000

£5,400 × 100/90

(2) The tax credit attaching to the dividend is:

£	600

£6,000 × 10%

(3) True ☐

False ✓

The tax credit cannot be repaid.

....

Task 5

	£
Salary (£7,500 × 12)	90,000
Bonus A (treated as received on 31 October 2015)	17,500
Bonus B (treated as received on 30 June 2016 – taxed in 2016/17)	0
Director's pension contribution (£90,000 × 5%)	(4,500)
Company's pension contribution (exempt benefit)	0
Company car benefit	3,250
Dividends (£3,800 × 100/90)	4,222
Interest from ISA	0
Net income	110,472
Personal allowance £(10,600 – ((110,472 – 100,000)/2))	5,364
Taxable income	105,108

Task 6

(a)

	£
Employment income	46,000
Bank interest £1,600 × 100/80	2,000
Dividends £4,500 × 100/90	5,000
	53,000
Personal allowance	(10,600)
Taxable income	42,400
Tax on non-savings income:	
£31,785 × 20%	6,357
£1,500 (£1,200 × 100/80) × 20%	300
£2,115 × 40% (£46,000 - £10,600 - £31,785 - £1,500)	846
Tax on savings income:	
£2,000 × 40%	800
Tax on dividend income:	
£5,000 × 32½ %	1,625
Income Tax Liability	9,928

(b) On which dates are payment on accounts due for 2015/16?

	✓
31 January 2016 and 31 July 2016	✓
31 January 2017 and 31 July 2017	
31 July 2016 and 31 January 2017	
31 October 2016 and 31 January 2017	

Payments on account are due on 31 January in the tax year and 31 July following the end of the tax year.

Task 7

(a)

	✓
National Crime Agency	✓
Association of Taxation Technicians	
Tax Tribunal	
HM Treasury	

(b)

Incorrect tax return

The maximum penalty for a careless (rather than a deliberate) error is 30% of the potential lost revenue (ie tax lost). Obviously this is only relevant if Jakki is a higher rate taxpayer, as the tax credit attaching to the dividend would cover her basic rate liability.

However, any penalty may be reduced to 0% if Jakki makes an unprompted disclosure. An unprompted disclosure is one made at a time when the taxpayer has no reason to believe HMRC has discovered, or is about to discover, the error. Jakki should therefore make disclosure to HMRC as soon as possible.

Task 8

Name	Gary Bryant
Box 1	27500.00
Box 2	4200.00
Box 5	HGK plc
Box 9	3200.00
Box 11	1500.00
Box 19	300.00

Task 9

(a)

Asset	Chargeable	Exempt
Horse		✓ (wasting asset)
Field in which horse is kept	✓	
Antique horse brass costing £500, worth £1,700		✓ (exempt chattel)

(b) The chargeable gain on sale is:

£	45,000

	£
Proceeds of sale	125,000
Less cost	(65,000)
enhancement expenditure	(15,000)
Chargeable gain	45,000

Redecoration is a revenue expense, not capital, and therefore not allowable.

(c) The allowable loss on sale is:

£	2,300

	£
Deemed disposal proceeds	6,000
Less disposal costs £(2,700 × 100/90) × 10%	(300)
Net proceeds	5,700
Less cost	(8,000)
Allowable loss	(2,300)

Task 10

Gain

	£
Proceeds of sale	8,000
Less cost	(1,250)
Chargeable gain	6,750

Share pool

	No of shares	Cost £
August 2009 Acquisition	2,000	5,000
September 2012 Bonus 1 for 1	2,000	0
	4,000	5,000
June 2015 Disposal (1,000/4,000 × £5,000)	(1,000)	(1,250)
c/f	3,000	3,750

Task 11

The CGT payable for 2015/16 is:

(a)

£	1,030

	£
Gains	15,100
Less annual exempt amount	(11,100)
Taxable gains	4,000

CGT

	£
£895 (W) × 18%	161
£3,105 × 28%	869
CGT	1,030

(W) Unused basic rate band is £31,785 + £500 (£400 × 100/80) – £31,390 = £895

(b) True ☐

False ☑

Provided the house has been occupied by the owner as his only or main residence at some time during the period of ownership, the last 18 months of ownership are exempt whether or not the owner lives in the house during that period.

TAXATION DATA

Taxation tables for personal tax – 2015/16

Note that 'TAXATION DATA 1' and 'TAXATION DATA 2' shown below will be available as pop-up windows throughout your live assessment.

TAXATION DATA 1

Pop-up 1

Tax rates and bands

	%	£
Basic rate	20	first 31,785
Higher rate	40	to 150,000
Additional rate	45	over 150,000

Savings income is taxed at 0%, 20%, 40% and 45%.

(0% applies to a maximum of £5,000 of savings income only where non-savings income is below this limit)

Dividends are taxed at 10%, 32.5% and 37.5%.

Personal allowances

	£
Personal allowance for individuals born after 5 April 1938	10,600
Age allowance for individuals born before 6 April 1938	10,660
Income limit for age allowance	27,700

TAXATION DATA 2

Pop-up 2

Car benefit percentage

Emission rating for petrol engines	%
0g/km to 50g/km	5
51g/km to 75g/km	9
76g/km to 94g/km	13
95g/km or more	14% + 1% for every extra 5g/km above 95g/km

Diesel engines – additional 3%

The figure for fuel is £22,100

Authorised mileage rates

First 10,000 miles	45p
Over 10,000 miles	25p

Van scale charge

	£
Charge	3,150
Private fuel provided	594
Zero emission van charge	630

HMRC official rate   3%

Capital gains tax

Annual exempt amount	£11,100
Tax rate	18%
Higher rate	28%